TOPIARY BASICS
THE ART OF SHAPING
PLANTS IN GARDENS
& CONTAINERS

To our children

ACKNOWLEDGMENTS

We would like to thank the following for their kind assistance in making their plants
available to the studio photographer: Breschi Nurseries, Effegarden, Oscar Tintori,
Vannucci Nurseries, and Anna Pejron Nursery.
For the tools: Mr. Ghedi of Agrimec-Farm Machinery.
For the pots: Curti Ceramics and Mati Nurseries.
Special thanks for valuable advice and suggestions go to: Franco Breschi, Enrico Cappellini,
Angelo Naj-Oleari, and Daniele Zanzi.
For information and addresses: Pius Floris and Professor Jette Abel.
In addition, thanks go to our respective spouses for their collaboration and to Enrico, who
on more than one occasion saved us from losing text in the mazes of the computer's
memory.

Photographic Credits:

Patrizia Bellei: pages 11, 26-27, 38-39, 47, 52-53, 115-126
Daniele Cavadini: pages 10, 14-15, 24-25, 60-61, 63, 124
Giustino De Lorenzo: pages 6-7, 28-29, 41, 79, 81
Ermes Lasagni: pages 8-9, 12-13, 16-17, 54, 55, 77, 116-117
Margherita Lombardi: pages 18, 20, 21, 22, 30, 31, 32-33, 46, 56, 57, 62, 64, 65, 76, 80, 107
Overseas: Ciprandi 37, Brenkle Explorer 23, 51, 69, Pigazzini 19, 127, Villorosa 58, 59

Editor: Cristina Sperandeo
Studio photography: Mario Matteucci
Drawings: Ilaria Lombardi
Translation: Rence Tannenbaum
Graphic design and layout: Paola Masera and Amelia Verga

Library of Congress Cataloging-in-Publication Data Available

10   9   8   7   6   5   4   3   2   1

First paperback edition published in 2001 by
Sterling Publishing Company, Inc.
387 Park Avenue South, New York, N.Y. 10016
First published in Italy by RCS Libri S.p.A.
Under the title *Topiaria e Sculture Verdi*
© 1999 by RCS Libri S.p.A.
English Translation © 1999 by Sterling Publishing Company, Inc.
Clare G. Harvey and Amanda Cochrane assert the moral right to be identified as the authors of this work.
Distributed in Canada by Sterling Publishing
℅ Canadian Manda Group, One Atlantic Avenue, Suite 105
Toronto, Ontario, Canada M6K 3E7
Distributed in Great Britain and Europe by Cassell PLC
Wellington House, 125 Strand, London WC2R 0BB, England
Distributed in Australia by Capricorn Link (Australia) Pty Ltd.
P.O. Box 704, Windsor, NSW 2756 Australia

Printed in China

Sterling ISBN 0-8069-3899-4 Trade
          0-8069-4171-5 Paper

Margherita Lombardi and Cristiana Serra Zanetti

TOPIARY BASICS
THE ART OF SHAPING PLANTS IN GARDENS & CONTAINERS

Sterling Publishing Co., Inc.
New York

Contents

Introduction

Topiary is the art of molding plants into geometric
or fantastic shapes. It dates back to the time of the Persians
and the ancient Greeks. No other style of gardening has
endured so long. Topiary art is fashionable once again
thanks, in part, to a renewed interest in historical gardens.
These gardens are being restored because of the high
quality of gardening they represent. Today, topiary art rarely
takes the form of labyrinths, elaborate parterres, and
other grand creations of the past; however, we find its
influences in fruit tree espaliers, formal hedges,
and large candelabra-shaped plane trees.

Topiary art is well suited to the modern garden and its
limited size. Hedges, borders, espaliers, arcades, and green
sculptures are elements that produce strong architectural and
decorative impact but create little clutter.

When used well, these elements allow you to divide space,
to highlight views and perspectives, and to reduce or
eliminate flaws. They decorate without overburdening;
they bestow a special quality; and they create an ordered
frame that both emphasizes and softens the luxuriance of the
other plants. This is in keeping with the architecture of the
modern home and of city balconies.

Nevertheless, topiary art can be a little daunting because we
associate it with large historical gardens, laborious upkeep,
and long years of waiting. In reality, this is not the case at
all, as we plan to demonstrate in this book. We are hoping
to provide a sense of the infinite number of possible shapes
and compositions and of the countless plants that you can
use, offering the basic technical knowledge you may need to
express and enjoy yourself with garden sculptures.

The style of the house, the surrounding landscape,
the climate, the time available, and personal taste will
suggest what may be done.

A History of Topiary Art

The origin of topiary art is buried in the darkness of time: a dizzying trail of green sculptures, geometric hedges, standards, espaliers, signs, prisms… a nearly endless history that, through the centuries, joins the gardens of Russell Page to Arab, Greek, and Roman gardens.

Topiaries in History

Today *ars topiaria*, the art of topiary, means the art of trimming and growing plants in geometric or fantastic shapes, but originally it had a different meaning. In fact, topiary art dates back to the ancient Greeks and their love of formality and order.

Ancient History

We believe that the Greeks learned this art in Persia after they conquered the region in the third century B.C. They were enchanted by the wonderful gardens in which hedges were formed by trimming myrtle and other shrubs into even shapes or by interweaving their branches. The origin of the word "topiary" is Greek. It is derived from *topia* or *topeia*, referring to the "cord" or "rope" used to tie the plants, or from *topos*, meaning "landscape." For the Greeks, and subsequently for the Romans, topiary art first consisted of making trompe l'oeils. *Topia* were paintings and bas-reliefs representing landscapes and plants. They were created on the walls of rooms and porticos to bring the garden into the house, thereby enlarging it. Trees, landscapes, rivers, seascapes, temples, and paintings in perspective on the outer wall created the illusion of greater depth and broader space.

*I*n the Boboli Garden, a high topiary hedge surrounds the large central fountain.

Later, to accentuate this effect, dwarf trees were planted in the background, exactly as the Japanese do today in their illusory gardens. The Greek word *topia* was used in its Latin form, *topiarius*, first to refer to the painter, then to the artist who specialized in reproducing landscapes in miniature. Eventually, this term was extended to the gardener who worked on ornamental gardens, as opposed to the *olitor*, *arborator*, and *vinitor*, terms that referred to those who grew vegetables, fruit trees, and vineyards. According to Cicero in 54 B.C., topiary was the art of making ivy and other plants climb on walls, columns, and terraces and of cutting trees and shrubs into different shapes. According to Pliny the Elder (23–79 A.D.), Caius Mattius, a nobleman and contemporary of Augustus, was the true inventor of the art of trimming trees and shrubs in even, decorative shapes. The plants most commonly used in that era were cypress, boxwood, holly, laurel, myrtle, rosemary, and ivy. These were used to make hedges, walls, espaliers, borders around flower beds, and, eventually, green sculptures in geometric shapes such as prisms, spheres, pyramids, and cones, as well as human and animal figures, gods, landscapes, and scenes of war and mythology.

In describing his own villa, Pliny the Younger (62–114 A.D.) spoke of the custom of writing the name of the homeowner or the creator of the garden in letters made of boxwood or other small shrubs. Among the many bizarre topiary creations reported was the amazing plane tree in Emperor Caligula's garden. The branches of the tree formed stands and steps on which at least fifteen people could sit around a table to eat. Julius Caesar and the great Roman territorial conquest spread topiary art and plants, such as cypress and boxwood, throughout Europe. However, as a result of the social chaos and instability that followed the fall of the Roman Empire, the art of topiary was almost lost, as was a great deal of gardening knowledge.

The Middle Ages

During the Middle Ages, topiary art survived only in the gardens of monasteries, convents, and castles. These gardens were small and enclosed, prototypes of the modern garden.

Geometric flower beds, divided into rectangular or circular sections, each dedicated to one type of cultivation and often with a small tree at the center, were bordered by low hedges of boxwood, santolina, teucrium, or other shrubs. The garden was predominantly productive, including roses, peonies, lilies, medicinal herbs, trees, and evergreen shrubs with medicinal or aromatic properties. Vegetables and fruit trees were grown in the flower beds. Only after the Middle Ages did topiary art reappear, initially in the form of hedges, screens, arbors, green arcades, and niches of lush greenery.

The garden of the Villa Gamberaia, in Settignano, is typical of a Renaissance garden; the space is divided into four flower beds with a circular fountain at the center.

The Renaissance

In the early fifteenth century, the high-class garden resembled the medieval garden: it was flat and even. Flowers, vegetables, and ornamental and medicinal plants grew indiscriminately; however, a uniform, geometric, and orderly design began to take shape as an architectural form. Topiary returned to its more imaginary shapes. Aromatic herbs and shrubs, such as boxwood, teucrium, juniper, and myrtle, were sculpted into spheres, stands, ships, temples, vases, jars, goblets, diamonds, elves, apes, dragons, camels, horses, donkeys, oxen, dogs, deer, bears, and pigs, as well as popes, cardinals, and other human figures. Espaliers, little huts or caves of juniper or boxwood, labyrinths, and signs with the name of the villa owner (similar to the ancient Roman ones) were also made during this period.

In the second half of the fifteenth century, the design and planting of small hedges, later referred to as "parterres," was a highly developed art form. Simple interwoven creations of fragrant herbs, such as marjoram, hyssop, rue, artemisia, teucrium, lavender, thyme, and nepeta, were made with small carnations, primroses, and violets planted within them. In addition, an elaborate topiary shape was usually placed at the center of the parterre as an element of relief.

In the sixteenth century, with the development of humanism and the rediscovery of classical literature, the supremacy of man over nature was affirmed. In his treatise of 1499, *Il sogno di un Polifilo*, Francesco Colonna wrote that man uses nature above all to define and structure space. This idea formed the foundation for European gardens for the next two centuries. Influenced by the gardens in the great Roman villas, the Renaissance garden represented a continuation of the concept of the open house. The Renaissance

*D*etail of the series of shapes that characterize the Villa Gamberaia.

garden tried to match the magnificence of those older gardens by following their architectural style and adding perspectives, terraces, ramps, and grand stairways dividing the property into even, geometric shapes.

Nothing could be left to chance; nature and plants were considered little more than building blocks to be retrained into the desired shapes. Evergreen plants were preferred because they

could be part of a year-round architectural composition. Trees such as cypress, pine, and holly were lined up along garden paths and in ordered thickets. Small-leaf shrubs such as boxwood, yew, myrtle, and laurel were molded into geometric shapes and used to create espaliers, borders, and green walls.

For the first time, people used wire frames to create more complicated shapes, intertwining the leafy branches of plants onto the iron wires. Large geometric or moderately elaborate embroidery designs were fashioned on terraces with small hedges of boxwood, teucrium, and other herbs. Flowering espaliers of citrus trees, pomegranate, laurel, myrtle, ivy, and honeysuckle, as well as rose and jasmine pergolas, lined the paths and hedges of the Renaissance garden.

The Seventeenth and Eighteenth Centuries

In the seventeenth century, the garden became an architectural, geometrical, and symmetrical composition. Several themes already present in the sixteenth century gained greater importance, for example, the green theater, the amphitheater, the parterre, and the labyrinth. However, at the same time, a liberating influence expressed itself in fantastic shapes modeled out of plants and in a greater emphasis on fusing the garden and its surrounding landscape. The taste for the pictorial was expressed alongside a tendency to grow plants in more natural shapes.

Among the examples of Italian gardens are the Villa Garzoni in Collodi and the Castello Balduino in Montalto. The first seems flowing and playful, with soft yew hedges, flower beds edged with boxwoods and dotted with geometric topiary shapes, and the more recently added animal shapes. In the second, large evergreen shrubs are cut in abstract and massive shapes and arranged according to a geometric design, harmonious but severe. In the eighteenth century and especially in the nineteenth century, French and English gardens were much admired. Many Italian parterres were destroyed and replaced with elaborate designs or irregular flower beds. One of the few surviving examples of the Italian parterre can still be admired at the Villa Ruspoli, in the region of Latium (Lazio). This garden dates back to the early eighteenth century. Increasingly elaborate parterres, arbors, shaded pathways with trees whose branches are interwoven, and large labyrinths characterized the Venetian gardens of the eighteenth and nineteenth centuries, while the Lombardy and Piedmont gardens demonstrated a great variety of styles because of their climate, topology, and location.

In large gardens, topiary heightens the impressive nature of the garden. In secluded spaces, topiary emphasizes the sense of intimacy.

France

Topiary art arrived in France with the Romans. It survived in the Middle Ages in the gardens of monasteries and castles, mirroring the evolution of the closed and protected upper-class garden in the fifteenth century.

France absorbed the taste for topiary art from Renaissance Italy but redefined it. French gardens were magnificent, vast in size, with an extensive use of fountains, canals, and waterways, as well as a large quantity of plants cut and molded to attest to man's supremacy over nature. Lines of trees and tall hedges underscored the long axial walkways and the precise, basic geometric design which was imposed on nature. Dating back to the late sixteenth century, gardener Claude Mollet and his father, Jacques, invented the *parterre en broderie*, or "embroidery on land," the prized designs created with dwarf boxwood hedges that represented a further elaboration of the even, geometric Renaissance flower beds. From *parterre en broderie* came the shortened term "parterre," commonly used to indicate the simpler Italian and English compositions. *Parterres en broderie* were rather typical of the more complex French style; they depicted emblems, initials, arabesques, and puzzles that could only be fully appreciated when viewed from above—from the residence's terraces or windows. Initially, the interior spaces of embroideries were filled with gravel and colored pebbles; later, medicinal herbs and seasonal flowers, such as tulips, narcissus, daisies, and violets, were used.

The French style was definitively established during the reign of the Sun King, Louis XIV, by André Le Nôtre, creator of the parks of Vaux-le-Vicomte and Versailles castles.

*J*oachim Carvallo, reproducing the characteristic elements of the French style, created the terraced garden at Villandry between 1906 and 1920.

André Le Nôtre

André Le Nôtre built a sumptuous garden in the park of the Vaux-le-Vicomte Castle. He used flat terraces dotted with large yew cones, boxwood spheres, detailed *parterres en broderie*, formal hedges, and endless rows of deciduous trees. The day after the park's opening celebration, the envious Sun King imprisoned the owner, charged

him with theft, and ordered Le Nôtre to create an even more beautiful garden for himself near Versailles. Thus, the giant park in Versailles was born. Its characteristic features would be copied in all the French and European gardens of the period.

Along with the classical plants of the topiary tradition, the French garden used a greater variety of plants and deciduous trees than was found in the typical Italian garden. For example, the French used hornbeam, elm, beech, maple, linden, plane, and horse chestnut trees. In fact, the impressive views that characterized these gardens demanded imposing arboreal masses, while the moderate brightness of the sky in north central France prevented the excessive use of evergreen plants, which would have looked too dark.

England

The Romans also brought topiary art to England. Although it nearly disappeared during the Middle Ages, it did continue in the gardens of monasteries, convents, and small country houses. Topiary gardens officially reappeared with the Norman Conquest and made their definitive mark after the Wars of the Roses (1455-1485), when more money was available. City gardens and large gardens on country estates were developed, inspired by the Italian Renaissance and filtered by French taste.

The "knot garden" was a characteristic element of the English garden. It was an elaboration of the parterre. More complex designs replaced simple-shaped flower beds. Sometimes, these were inspired by Celtic motifs. Two hedges, one of boxwood and the other usually teucrium, were pruned in such a way as to seem to intersect and to intertwine. At first, the space left free of "knots" was filled with pebbles or colored earth. Later, the space was used for plants of contrasting colors, such as lavender, rue, and rosemary. The "knot garden" was most widespread in the seventeenth century, especially in Scotland under the reign of James VI (1566–1625). The golden age of the English garden and of the topiary garden in particular coincided with the Tudor period (1485–1603). This was the period when an English style was established. Although influenced by the Italian

Detail of the garden at Sissinghurst Castle showing how two boxwood spheres accentuate the passageway, inviting the visitor to walk through it.

and French styles, the English style did not reach the grandeur of its predecessors, not even in the most important gardens. In the Tudor garden, topiary became mostly a structural element used to define a series of outdoor "rooms" by means of formal hedges and rows of interwoven trees. The hedge, in particular, was used to define borders, divide space, protect the more delicate species of plants, and enhance the flowers. It was found everywhere, in large as well as small gardens, in vegetable gardens, in rose gardens, and in both herbaceous and aromatic herb gardens. Holly, yew, boxwood, laurel, cherry laurel, phillyrea, teucrium, santolina, maple, beech, and hornbeam were used for hedges, knot parterres, labyrinths, arches, and geometric and fantastic green sculptures. The yew, introduced as a topiary plant in Holland and England in the second half of the seventeenth century, was widely used and preferred to the boxwood because it was larger and hardier. Topiary art reached its peak between 1689 and 1702, during the reign of William of Orange, who brought the nearly unrestrained use of topiary figures from Holland.

Especially in Scotland, strange and absurd green sculptures were created, such as centaurs, mermaids, servant girls, crowns, dragons, small constructions with doors and windows, battle scenes, or other historical events.

At right, the extraordinary topiary structures of the eighteenth-century garden at Levens Hall have survived unchanged.

In Fingask, Scotland, 250 cone-shaped yew trees serve as a counterpoint to a multitude of statues. At Brickwall in Sussex, topiary figures recreate a chess game. The Yew Garden at Packwood House, in Warwickshire, portrays the Sermon on the Mount. The Twelve Apostles, with a multitude of followers at their feet, are represented at Cleeve Prior at Eversham.

In the eighteenth century, the tendency to shape plants in an artistic fashion to achieve fantastic results was pursued to absurd lengths. The garden became a kind of playground for nobility and the sovereign. Increasingly elaborate hedges and labyrinths and entire menageries of animals and other strange things were sculpted, provoking reactions that evolved into a true rebellion against topiary art. This gave birth to a movement to return to nature. Many English topiary gardens were destroyed in the late eighteenth century; they were transformed into "country gardens." Later, many European gardens suffered a similar fate. One of the few remaining examples of extraordinary English topiary work, similar to abstract sculpture, is the garden of Levens Hall, in Westmorland. Despite almost total opposition, topiary art continued to surface in the form of small creations in private gardens until the late eighteenth and early nineteenth centuries, when it reappeared in large gardens in the form of geometric hedges, espaliers, and green sculptures. In the second half of the

*T*he garden at Sissinghurst Castle, an example of how after the 1920s, a simplified English topiary was used in the garden. This one is divided into "rooms."

nineteenth century, the formal evergreen and dark green hedge became a precious element for the development of the "mixed border" conceived by Gertrude Jeckyll. The brilliant uniformity of the yew tree formed a background enhancing the beauty of the foliage and the flowers.

Topiary has had several fierce enemies, hostile at least to its more obvious eccentricities. For example, William Robinson, creator of the native herbaceous border, compared the art of shaping plants to the Oriental custom of binding women's feet. After World War One, English topiary became simpler, but yew and boxwood hedges continued to form the architectural structure of country house gardens. The "garden room" style reappeared and developed further. You can see wonderful examples of this style in the gardens of Tintinhull, Sissinghurst Castle, and Hidcote Manor. The style is similar to that of the ancient Spanish-Arabic gardens.

Today, topiary is primarily used to create borders and dividing hedges, green arcades, fruit tree espaliers, and ornamental shrubs. Small geometric shapes, such as spheres, cones, and pyramids, are also popular for corners, for areas beside borders and doors, and for pots to decorate paved areas. Real and imaginary creatures are used to soften the severity of a hedge.

*A*t right, a detail of the Sissinghurst Castle garden, where high hornbeam and yew hedges divide the space into many "rooms."

Holland

Topiary art was established in Holland as far back as the twelfth century. It was well suited to the country's need to design gardens in restricted spaces. The Dutch style decisively influenced the English style towards the end of the seventeenth century. This is obvious in the widespread use of the yew trimmed in a geometric shape. The Dutch style left its mark on the French and Italian styles as well, but to a lesser degree.

The Spanish-Arabic Garden

Topiary established its own style in Spain and Portugal, but these styles did not influence other countries in a major way. The Spanish garden was closed and secret, tightly connected to the house – a descendant of the Roman atrium and medieval cloister. In the north, there was something of the preciousness and order of the French garden, but without its magnificence. The Moorish heritage, with its linear orientation, simplicity, and sense of intimacy and peace, was the dominant influence. Boxwood, myrtle, laurel, and cypress were grown in simple geometric shapes and in trimmed hedges. The aim was perfect symmetry of place, as in the Cuarto de Comares in the gardens of the Alhambra. The typical flower bed, filled with free-growing shrubs, bordered by a formal boxwood hedge, recalls English gardens of the twentieth century, such as Hidcote Manor and Sissinghurst Castle.

*T*ulips and topiary provide color and linear orientation in the garden of Keukenhoff in Holland.

Portugal

Portugal elaborated on the Roman, Arabic, Italian, Renaissance, and baroque styles. Topiary was used in abundance, as is obvious in the numerous surviving gardens, but in Portugal it differed in its unusual plants and unique shapes. True, it used rather simple parterres and flower beds bordered with boxwood, arches, arcades, and geometric shapes, such as prisms, pyramids, spheres, and cylinders. However, we also find wavy hedges enriched with decorative elements, flowered parterres, and very elaborate shapes in exquisite baroque style. Typical features of Portuguese gardens were the umbrella-shaped evergreen trees that provided shaded sitting areas and the division of the garden into enfilade: a series of rooms that open onto one another through large windows, arches, and doors cut into the greenery. Another characteristic feature, which was nearly lost, especially in northern gardens such as the garden at the Royal Villa of Mateus, was the use of tall arcades made from cypress trees. These were trimmed by gardeners lying on top of large, semicircular ladders. Portuguese topiary art is also unique for its use of the camellia, which grows well in the mild, cool, and airy climate. The camellia transforms hedges, arches, small constructions, and various other sculptures into extraordinary flowering mosaics.

*A*t right, the nearly exclusive use of evergreens is typical of the Portuguese garden.

Other Countries

Towards the end of the Renaissance, topiary art became known throughout the rest of Europe. The French style, with its magnificence and widespread use of characteristic deciduous plants, became the standard. Topiary shapes very similar to those of the French appeared in large Belgian gardens as tall, long walls of hornbeam. There were examples of interwoven rows of trees, such as the row of field maples at Schönbrunn Castle in Austria, while in Germany, the espalier, candelabra-shaped trees, and green arcades were most widespread. In the seventeenth century, Scandinavian gardeners pruned boxwood and hawthorn hedges into geometric shapes, but it was not until the eighteenth century that the art of topiary figured prominently in the architecture of Scandinavian gardens. During the baroque period, the Danes used boxwood to create *parterre de broderie.* They used yews for labyrinths and green theaters, linden trees for "raised hedges," and candelabra shapes, exedrae, and outdoor benches for resting in the shade. At the end of the seventeenth century, topiary art became widespread in the United States. However, it was only in the eighteenth century, after the country acquired a certain political and economic stability, that large gardens were created. The strong appeal that European culture wielded over the United States generated the creation of various public and private reconstructions of topiary gardens from the past, with parterres, labyrinths, and green sculptures. The most extraordinary of topiary collections is located in the Green Animals garden in Portsmouth, Rhode Island, created between 1905 and 1940 by Joseph Carriero. It has an incredible zoo, inspired by the Roman and Italian tradition. The garden features giraffes, elephants, lions, camels, unicorns, peacocks, reindeer, and many more animals. Most were sculpted in privet with the help of metal frames. The collection in Ladew

A precise reconstruction of a Japanese garden in Disneyland.

Gardens in Maryland is very similar. This garden specializes in boxwood topiaries including a famous fox hunt with dogs, foxes, and riders on horseback portrayed in the act of jumping over a hurdle. Imaginative and animated green sculptures have even found a home in Disney World. American topiary art has also been influenced by the Japanese. In particular, American topiary art assimilated their use of growing and pruning plants in cloud shapes with highly effective architectural results. The most

widely used plants are the privet, pyracantha, fruit trees, boxwood, yew, the *Magnolia grandiflora* (though it has climatic limits), and climbing plants, especially ivy.

For green sculptures, American topiary generally uses metal structures and frames, employing climbing plants and shrubs.

Over the centuries, topiary art has spread throughout the world, reaching Peter the Great's Russia and China, where, in the eighteenth century, the emperor Quian Long had a garden made in the French style with labyrinths, parterres, and green sculptures.

Among examples of exotic topiary, the most spectacular is certainly the cemetery of Tulcán, in northern Ecuador, with its series of animal, geometric, and anthropomorphic figures in the pre-Colombian style.

The group of sculptures, chiseled in a long hedge of *Cupressus arizonica*, was designated a national monument in 1984, just over twenty years after it was begun.

Contemporary Topiary Art

Although topiary shapes rarely dominate modern gardens, labyrinths and parterres in historical gardens are today being restored. Topiary art, however, has pervaded gardening and horticulture to such an extent that it is often represented unconsciously in large and small gardens. For example, we are using the art of topiary each time we trim a fruit tree in a set shape, prune a hedge, or create a pergola. Famous landscapers, such as Russell Page and Pietro Porcinai, base their projects on the art of topiary, or at least they include some elements. With the excesses of French grandeur and the search for English intimacy abandoned, topiary now explores its functional role of defining and highlighting the presence of nature in the garden.

The size of the contemporary garden (too narrow for the typical country-style garden and too difficult for masking boundaries) and the thickness of the plants used have recently restored the original structural function to the art of topiary. In fact, topiary is perfect for small spaces where, with the skillful use of hedges and espaliers, it can create a permanent structure that is decorative even without its seasonal flowers. A boxwood ball, a spiral or a cone shaped out of yew or laurel, a small dwarf boxwood parterre, or an espalier in just the right spot can lend an ancient flavor and provide adequate screening with delicacy and geometry.

Russell Page designed many gardens in Italy and southern France. These gardens demonstrate the successful combination of Mediterranean plants, herbs, and traditional topiaries in a strong modern style by playing on the large-scale repetition of a geometric design and by using plants in bunches. An excellent example of his elegant and steady style is the Gardens of Landriana in Tor San Lorenzo near Rome, which is divided by flowering paths into many formal and informal gardens, such as the Giardino degli Ulivi (Olive Garden) and the Giardino degli Aranci (Orange Garden).

In the Garden and in Pots

Topiary art is extremely well suited to the modern garden. It can create a decorative composition, define borders, divide, and screen. Using topiary in containers is effective in courtyards and on balconies to ornament limited spaces with lasting decorative motifs.

Topiary in the Garden

Topiary art is a term that probably brings to mind an image of large Italian gardens, elaborate French parterres, or endless divided English hedges. That may be a bit intimidating. In reality, topiary art appears even in very small gardens much more often than one might believe.

The simplest privet hedge is an example of topiary if it is trimmed in a geometric or imaginary shape. But topiary, without attempting to copy the grand creations of the past, offers a lot to large and small gardens, even to balconies. With a little imagination and a little architectural sensitivity, anyone possessing botanical or gardening knowledge can enjoy shaping plants.

Topiary art is suited to the small modern garden, resolving the problems of defining boundaries and distributing plants, and allowing the creation of a decorative composition for all seasons. But the same holds true for medium and large gardens. In these larger spaces, the elements of surprise and intimacy can be introduced by dividing spaces with hedges, espaliers, and screens into smaller spaces. The sequence of green, open "rooms" is a source of interest and decoration. This prevents the visitor from seeing the whole garden in one glance, arouses a taste for discovery, and expands its actual size. Each room can be "furnished" in its own way, experimenting with different styles and different plants. You can create a White Garden, a Blue Garden, a Rose Garden, an Herb Garden, and an herbaceous border without connecting any of the rooms stylistically. For example, a small collection of roses in a space defined by a formal evergreen hedge will look neat and will preserve its decorative value even during the winter months. On the other hand, an architectural solution does not prevent you from creating a garden with a naturalistic character, since the variety of plants will tone down the geometric effect.

A small boxwood sphere is enough to lend structure and order to a composition of plants.

At right, the abundance of colorful blossoms softens the geometric severity of the flower bed.

Contemporary Gardens

In a few modern topiary gardens, the precision and rigidity of the architecture harmonizes perfectly with the clean lines of the plants. In a rather small space, ordered, geometric elements help to tone down the impression of bareness and emptiness that can characterize the garden during the winter months. Simple geometric flower beds, bordered by a dwarf boxwood hedge with a boxwood pyramid, cone, or sphere at each corner, can decorate the garden elegantly, bestowing character and order. These also work well with brick, tile, or gravel walkways, further reducing the necessary upkeep.

The idea of creating a topiary garden may be intimidating when you think of the years needed to achieve the desired forms and of the frequent trimming. In reality, the initial waiting period is comparable to that of an informal garden. Once the plants have reached maturity, it is much simpler to maintain the balance of a topiary garden than that of an informal garden with its varying plant growth. You can reduce the time that the plants and the shapes need to reach maturity by buying plants that are already a certain size or by using structures.

In addition to hedges, espaliers, and rows of plants, whose functions are structural first and then decorative, topiary art offers countless solutions for the contemporary garden: spheres, cones, pyramids, cylinders, cubes, and spirals suitably positioned become discrete, but efficient, focal points.

With topiary, you can design a variety of neat frames around an arrangement of your favorite plants. In fact, a few simple elements are enough to achieve something special, even in a small space.

The Plan

Before starting to plant, you must have a plan to follow. In order to select the plants and to determine the kind of composition to use, you'll need some preliminary information on the nature of the soil, the climate, and the exposure.

To determine the best plan, observe the location, the residence, and the surrounding environment. Topiary is particularly successful when it echoes the architecture of the house or the surrounding environment. Every garden is rich in ideas suited to topiary, depending on the style of the dwelling, the location, the surrounding landscape, the presence of a wall, pavement, or other particular features. If there is a panorama, a view, or an interesting perspective, you should take advantage of it by designing the garden in such a way as to open up the view with a walkway, an arch, or a window in the hedge. Because gardens, especially topiary ones, last a long time, during the planning stage you need to imagine how the plants will grow over a span of twenty or even fifty years, especially the hedges and the structural elements. To make a plan, you need to identify the boundaries and the axes of the garden, the views, and the paths. Then you can divide the remaining space into geometric shapes, such as circles, rectangles, squares, or triangles, to form the basic design. You position the border hedges and the inner hedges to serve as structural separations or to emphasize the division of space. The hedges protect what they enclose and conceal their contents by directing attention elsewhere.

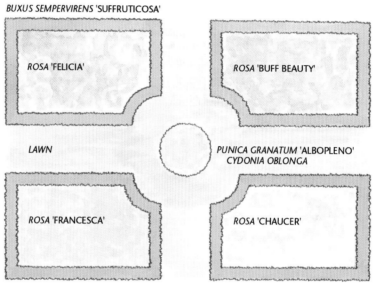

BUXUS SEMPERVIRENS 'SUFFRUTICOSA'

ROSA 'FELICIA'

ROSA 'BUFF BEAUTY'

LAWN

PUNICA GRANATUM 'ALBOPLENO'
CYDONIA OBLONGA

ROSA 'FRANCESCA'

ROSA 'CHAUCER'

Boxwood hedges and reflowering roses are a traditional choice.

They also obstruct the view. You can alter the shape of the garden by where you place a hedge. For example, you can transform a long, narrow, rectangular garden by planting a hedge halfway down the garden, joining the two vertical sides horizontally, and then carving out a small opening (a window, arch, or small door) to provide a glimpse of the other side. On the other hand, you can make a square garden appear deeper with a hedge along each of the two vertical sides or with a hedge on one side, forming a narrow green corridor. Avoid very high and voluminous hedges in small gardens, where they take up too much space and overwhelm the garden. In large gardens, however, these can bestow grandeur and importance. Within each space, you can give way to indulgence and plant whatever you like. You may choose a small parterre of herbs, a rose, lavender, or

perennial herbaceous border, a hazelnut or laburnum arcade, a small arbor, an archway framing the surrounding scenery, a pyracantha or fruit tree espalier, or a raised hornbeam hedge. In a rectangular or circular flower bed or in a small boxwood parterre animated with spheres, pyramids or spirals, you can grow lettuce, cauliflower, and seasonal flowers since the design will remain decorative even after you harvest them. In a city garden, a pool of still water can reflect a dwarf boxwood hedge, enclosing and decorating it over the winter. Finally, consider paving stones or bricks surrounding a boxwood or lavender border filled with grass or perennial flowers, such as forget-me-nots, veronica, or violets. Where space is limited, a boxwood sphere alone can highlight the roundness of a group of hosta or the vertical lines of several tall herbaceous plants, such as lupine and foxglove.

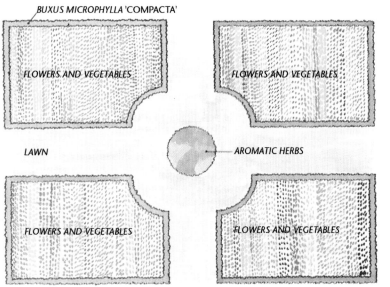

BUXUS MICROPHYLLA 'COMPACTA'

FLOWERS AND VEGETABLES

FLOWERS AND VEGETABLES

LAWN

AROMATIC HERBS

FLOWERS AND VEGETABLES

FLOWERS AND VEGETABLES

Low boxwood hedges or hedges of herbs, vegetables, and flowers frame a kitchen garden, as an alternative, rows of herbaceous plants.

Choosing Plants

The success of a garden depends on choosing the right plants for the specific climate, soil, and exposure. These elements strongly influence the development of the garden.

Before deciding on which plants and how to grow them, you need to know how long winter lasts, the minimum and maximum temperatures, whether or not there are late frosts, how and when it rains, if there are strong winds, and if and when it snows. Remember that a wall, hedge, or building can actually create a different climate. Any of these elements can provide protection from the wind or from excessive exposure to the sun. For example, city gardens and balconies, especially those with southern exposures, are always more sheltered and, thus, are favorable for growing less hardy species.

Shade and sun are not constant during the course of the year, in a garden or on a balcony. Southern exposures, suited to the cultivation of semi-hardy or tender species, can, during warm periods, cause plants to scorch and dry out. Western exposures are the safest because they are in shade in the early hours of the morning but in the sun during the rest of the day. Eastern exposures, which are sunny in the morning, can become too shady for tight, dense growth, limiting the flowering of many species. In locations that are subject to late frosts, there is the risk of damage to the buds, flowers, and leaves of evergreen and early-blooming species.

All topiary plants grow best in the sun. However, some species can tolerate shade, while others refuse to bloom in it. In general, evergreen species, especially yew and holly, develop well in the shade. If the shade is light and intermittent, their foliage assumes a more intense and richer color. The varieties with variegated, silvery, light blue, and golden leaves acquire sharper colors in the sun, while in the shade they tend to turn green.

Despite appearances, many plant species are so flexible that they lend themselves to countless original shapes of topiary art.

Buying Plants

Always choose healthy and well-shaped plants. The development of the top part must be symmetrical, with a balanced structure. Hedge plants should have good lower and side branches. For quick growth, they should also show a well-formed central shoot. For growing hedges, use young plants because they withstand transplanting better and grow faster than older ones. For all plants, the foliage should be the proper color and size, without any yellowing, dry parts, or parasites. The roots are healthy if they are light in color, firm, and moist. When dead, they are dark, fragile, dry, and limp. They also should be free of mold, larvae, or other parasites.

Soil and Drainage

The majority of the species used in topiary can adapt to any kind of soil, provided that it is fertile and well drained. Of course, plants will grow more or less lushly depending on how much the soil differs from ideal soil characteristics. If, however, the soil has very distinct qualities, such as being very acidic or showing the presence of limestone, you need to choose plants that do well in that kind of environment. Obviously, you must know your own soil. You should collect a 2-pound (1-kg) sample, or more if the soil does not seem homogenous, by digging a 6- to 8-inch (15- to 20-cm) hole. Have the sample analyzed. If the soil characteristics—structure, acidity, limestone content, depth, or drainage—are very far from average, you'll need to correct the problems with the help of a specialist. For good plant development, you'll want to improve clayish and heavy soils by adding sand, peat, and organic matter. For overly sandy and loose soil, you'll want to add organic matter.

Heavy soil or soil with too much clay has the disadvantage of being cold, causing plants to grow more slowly. This soil is difficult to work and tends to retain water too long, a condition that facilitates the onset of very serious root rot. On the other hand, sandy soil warms up quickly, but loses water just as quickly. It tends to be arid and poor in nutritional substances.

You also need to pay a great deal of attention to drainage. If the soil stays saturated with water, or if a layer of clay prevents the proper circulation of water, the roots may be asphyxiated, and the plants will die.

The theater of greenery made of tall yew, laurel, and hornbeam hedges is a typical feature of the Renaissance garden. Notice the statues placed in niches at the Villa Reale Marlia, Lucca.

Potted Topiaries

You can also train topiary plants to grow in pots. Pruning them helps them grow in containers because it limits root development.

Potted topiaries find a perfect home on balconies, in courtyards, and on patios, where they take up little space and, if they are evergreen, maintain their decorative value throughout the year. A couple of small boxwoods in the shape of spirals or balls, placed on either side of a door, or a group of different shapes in a corner are enough to provide an old, traditional feel. However, they are just as decorative in a garden when used to accentuate important points, stairways, and portals. For example, four pyramid-shaped boxwoods placed at either side of the entrance invite the visitor to enter; two small spheres framing a bench emphasize the sense of intimacy; a pair of spirals at the end of a pergola or a green covered walkway increases the sense of depth; a row of different shapes made from the same species arranged at the base of a hedge enriches it by underscoring its linear quality.

Small evergreen topiaries grown in pots and

*A*bove, handmade Lombard terra-cotta pot. Below, planters made of treated birch.

*A*t right, potted topiaries, highly decorative in the garden, create focal points.

pruned in simple, geometric shapes suit any kind of garden, be it romantic, formal, or modern in style. Use the shapes of birds, baskets, or topiaries that reproduce actual objects with greater discretion. They are entertaining, especially for children, but can become tiresome over time. Place these kinds of topiary in slightly hidden positions, not where they draw attention. Due to their unnatural rigidity, topiaries on frames in shapes such as a standard ball, cone, pyramid, or spiral covered with climbers like ivy, *Ficus pumila*, and *Muehlenbeckia* are better grown in pots and placed near the house than planted directly in the garden.

The choice of a pot is very important. Given its decorative function, the pot must be pleasant to look at, simple with a certain uniqueness, and a suitable match for the color of the foliage and the shape of the plant it will hold. Also consider the style of the garden and the architecture of the house. You can use stone or terra-cotta containers that are simple or decorated, half barrels, or wooden vats. Be sure to choose pots that are the right size for the development of the plants. Larger is better in order to minimize the need for repotting the plant. Pay special attention to the soil; it must be rich in organic matter and well drained. Place a layer of pebbles, gravel, porous clay pellets, or terra-cotta pieces in the bottom of the pot to hold the necessary water. The pot must also have drainage holes to allow the excess water to drain off. Before potting, immerse terra-cotta and wooden containers in water so that they don't absorb moisture from the soil. Like all potted plants, topiaries require more frequent watering than plants in the ground do. Use enough fertilizer to keep the soil fertile and to ensure an efficient growth, but don't overdo it. Use a slow-releasing fertilizer in the fall or at the beginning of spring.

Evergreens and flowering plants trained into standards are particularly ornamental.

Shapes

Using topiary art, man has
modeled shapes of every kind,
from simple and geometric
to very elaborate
and bizarre.

Parterres

The custom of creating elaborate flower beds with small boxwood hedges or herbs is one of the oldest expressions of topiary art. These flower beds were part of medieval gardens, just as they are part of contemporary gardens. They are suitable for cultivating vegetables, herbs, flowers, and fruit trees.

In Italian Renaissance gardens, the parterre was simple and severe. It became much more complicated and played on different shades of green and gray in the knot gardens of Tudor England. The French embroidered it as if it were a flowered tapestry in their grandiose gardens. The parterre still exists in large and small contemporary gardens everywhere, adapting itself to every type of situation. Parterres can be of different styles and sizes, according to the architecture of the house and the available space. In rectangular or square flower beds, for example, you can create a small kitchen garden, growing herbs or vegetables and small fruit trees. A simple geometric boxwood parterre, with perhaps a sphere, a cone, or a spiral at each corner, brings order and color throughout the year. In addition, it creates a background for the flowers and foliage of the other plants with its quiet, yet changing, green tones. You can grow roses, lavender, or perennial evergreen plants.

*T*he green of the boxwood creates a permanent background for flowering annuals at the Boboli Garden.

You might want only a single species, or you might prefer a variety. You could also use a perfectly mowed grass lawn. In addition, you can fill the interior space with rocks, sand, or colored earth. You can place grass, gravel, or a brick or stone pavement around it, thus simplifying the upkeep. In order to create an actual knot garden, without the complex design of the sixteenth and seventeenth centuries, we suggest that you use only two or three different species, with foliage of contrasting colors. You might want to try the dwarf boxwood, which requires more time to grow but less pruning than, for example, santolina. Trace the design on a piece of paper; choose the position of each small hedge to give the illusion that the different plants are interwoven. When you do the actual planting, copy the design on the ground using sand, and work from the outside inward.

*T*o the right, the parterre of the garden of the Villa Giusti in Verona.

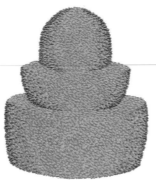

Hedges

Formally trimmed hedges are the most common expression of topiary art, but we rarely identify them as such. Hedges have many functions. For example, the outer ones emphasize the boundaries of a property, forming an ideal background for shrubs and borders, defining the proportions and architectural configuration of the garden.

Hedges separate the property from the outside world; they protect and hide it, creating intimacy. They also shelter it from the wind, reducing evaporation in the soil and allowing the cultivation of otherwise less hardy plants. Less costly than walls and fences and more pleasing to the eye, hedges also represent an ideal background for clumps of shrubs and especially for herbaceous borders. Above all, hedges define the proportions and architectural configuration of

the garden; depending on their height, thickness, and position, they alter the garden's appearance. A hedge placed halfway down the garden, joining two vertical sections, can shorten a long and narrow garden, while a hedge on each vertical side of a square or very wide garden

Depending on the style of the garden, you can enliven the longest hedges with arches, windows, openings, and topiary shapes. You can also carve battlements or waves.

emphasizes its depth. A very tall and wide hedge does not work well in a small garden, taking up too much space from the other plants, making them look cramped. On the other hand, it works well in a large garden, which accentuates its imposing nature. In addition, hedges allow you to divide the garden into many smaller gardens, creating secluded places and secret corners that appear unexpectedly. To highlight the sense of intimacy and surprise, you can carve out arches, doors, and windows that open onto charming foreshortened views of the garden itself or onto the surrounding landscape. Depending on your goal, hedges can be higher or lower, thicker or thinner. They range in size from the 8–12 inch (20–30 cm) dwarf boxwood hedge in parterres and knot gardens to the enormous, impenetrable walls of yew, beech, and hornbeam that are at least 3 feet (1 m) wide. They can be simple, square, rectangular, rounded, curving, or rolling. Their sides can be perpendicular, tapered, or shaped to echo the architecture of the house or a nearby building. You can make battlements, arches, spheres, cubes, cones, animals, and other shapes. You can create niches in which to put statues or plants of focal interest, or you can use hedges to frame or point out a particular decoration. You can also break up a very long hedge by placing small hedges alongside it at regular intervals. When a small hedge is placed

perpendicular to the long one, the intersection creates rooms where you can grow plants that require sheltered positions. Another type of hedge, similar to a row of trees, is the raised hedge (also called the peaked hedge). Here, you shape the foliage into a square, starting from a certain height on the bare trunks. This hedge is very useful for defining corridors and creating interesting plays of greenery with the leaves of other hedges or individual plants. The function dictates whether you need evergreen or deciduous plants, fast- or slow-growing plants, large, medium, or small plants (as long as they can withstand continuous trimming). Border hedges, for example, should be high, thick, and impenetrable. Therefore, we usually create them with vigorous species, such as yew, holly, *Berberis*, *Thuja*, *Chamaecyparis*, beech, hornbeam, field maple, hawthorn, *Pyracantha*, *Cotoneaster*, and in mild climates, laurel and *Ilex*. To enliven a very long hedge, you can mix different plants, evergreens and deciduous, such as holly, boxwood, hornbeam, beech, and yew. You can also alternate the plants of one species, for example, holly, boxwood, euonymus, privet, or honeysuckle, with its golden, silvery, or variegated varieties, creating subtle plays of color. The green-leaf species or varieties are hardier; plant fewer of them so that they do not overwhelm the variegated or colored-leaf plants.

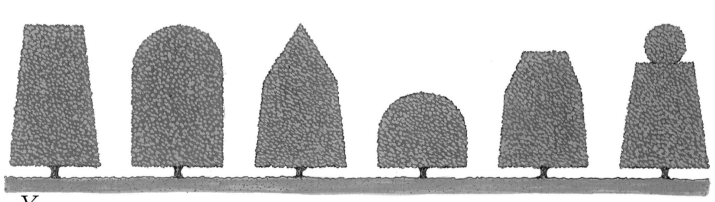

*Y*ou can shape hedges in different ways: parallel sided, wavy, rounded, pointed, or adorned with battlements and decorative elements on the top.

*T*o support the natural development of the plant, the base must be wider than or equal to the top.

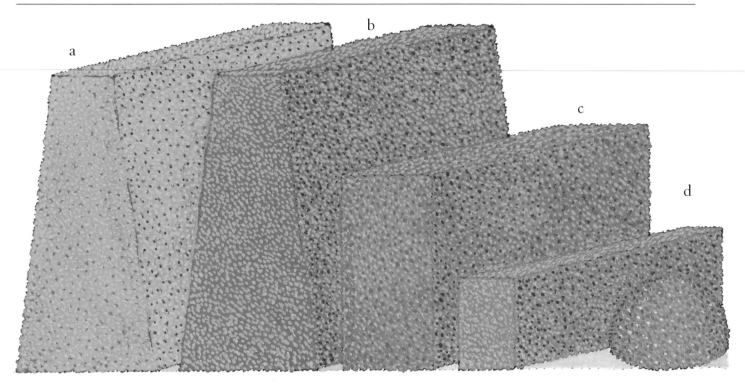

a- HEDGES OF 12–18 FEET
(400–600 cm) AND OVER

1. Acer campestre
2. Carpinus betulus
3. Chamaecyparis sp.
4. Crataegus sp.
5. Cupressocyparis leylandii
6. Cupressus sempervirens
7. Fagus sylvatica
8. Ilex acquifolium
9. Ligustrum
10. Laurus nobilis
11. Magnolia grandiflora
12. Pittosporum tenuifolium
13. Quercus ilex
14. Taxus baccata
15. Thuya sempervirens
16. Tsuga canadenis

b- HEDGES OR ESPALIERS OF
6–12 FEET (200–400 cm)

1. Acer campestre
2. Arbutus unedo
3. Camelia sp.
4. Carpinus betulus
5. Chamaecyparis sp.
6. Cupressocyparis sp.
7. Cupressus sempervirens
8. Cotoneaster 'Cornubia', C. franchetii,
C. lacteus, C. salicifolius
9. Crataegus sp.
10. Eleagnus x ebbingei, E. pungens
11. Euonymus japonicus
12. Fagus sylvatica
13. Ilex aquifolium
14. Laurus nobilis
15. Ligustrum ovalifolium, L. sinense,
L. vulgare, L. japonicum, L. ionandrum

16. Magnolia grandiflora
17. Pittosporum
18. Osmanthus fragrans
19. Osmanthus x fortunei
20. Osmanthus heterophyllus
21. Quercus ilex
22. Viburnum tinus

c- HEDGES OR ESPALIERS OF
$2\frac{1}{2}$–6 FEET (80–200 cm)

1. Arbutus unedo, A.u. 'Compacta'
2. Berberis aggregata, B. candidula,
B. darwinii, B. thunbergii, B. x
ottawensis, B. rubrostilla B. wilsoniae
3. Buxus microphilla 'Sunnyside'
4. Buxus sempervirens 'Suffruticosa',
B. s. 'Elegans', B. s. 'Faulkner',
B. s. 'Fiesta', B. s. 'Handsworthensis'
5. Camellia sp.
6. Cotoneaster 'Cornubia', C. franchetii,
C. lacteus, C. salicifolius
7. Euonymus japonicus
8. Juniperus sp.
9. Laurus nobilis
10. Ilex aquifolium
11. Ligustrum ovalifolium, L. sinense,
L. vulgare, L. japonicum, L. ionandrum
12. Lonicera nitida, L. pileata
13. Myrtus communis, M. tarantina,
M. apiculata
14. Olearia x scillonensis, O. solandri
15. x Osmarea burkwoodii
16. Osmanthus delavayi, O. fragrans,
O. fortunei, O. heterophyllus
17. Phillyrea angustifolia, P. decora
18. Pittosporum tenuifolium, P. ralphii,
P. crassifolium, P. tobira
19. Prunus laurocerasus 'Herbergii',

P. l. 'Schipkaensis', P. lusitanica
20. Pyracantha angustifolia, P. coccinea
21. Teucrium fruticans
22. Viburnum propinquum, V. tinus
23. Taxus baccata
24. Thuya plicata

d- BORDERS OF 8 INCHES – $2\frac{1}{2}$
FEET (20–80 cm)

1. Buxus microphylla 'Compacta',
B. m 'Koreana', B. m. 'Morris Midget',
B. m. 'Sunnyside'
2. Buxus sempervirens 'Suffruticosa'
3. Berberis thunbergii 'Atropurpurea
Nana', B.rubrostilla, B. wilsoniae
4. Eounymus officinalis.
5. Hyssopus officinalis
6. Lavandula angustifolia, L. stoechas,
L. dentata
7. Lonicera nitida, L. pileata
8. Myrtus communis
9. Olearia x hastii, O. nummularifolia,
O. 'Waikariensis'
10. Osmanthus delavayi
11. Osmarea x burkwoodii
12. Phillirea angustifolia, P. decora
13. Pittosporum tobira 'Nanum'
14. Prunus laurocerasus 'Otto Luyken'
15. Salvia officinalis
16. Santolina chamaecyparissus e S. virens
17. Senecio maritima, S.monroi,
S. 'Sunshine'
18. Thymus vulgaris

Shaped hedges emphasize the long grassy path at the Manoir d'Erygnac Salignac Garden in France's Dordogne Valley.

Labyrinths

The origin of the labyrinth has been lost in the darkness of time. Be it an ornamental puzzle, initiation rite, or metaphorical and magical symbol, we find labyrinths associated with most ancient peoples. It was also adapted by the followers of Christianity as a symbol of man's winding journey towards the truth.

Originally made of stone and bricks, since the Middle Ages the labyrinth has been composed of vegetable plants in the cloisters of monasteries. Monks walked along these twisted pathways to learn the virtues of constancy and patience. At first, the pathways were made of cut grass. Later they were defined by lavender, teucrium, thyme, hyssop, and dwarf boxwood borders. From the Renaissance onward, the hedges grew taller and taller, until they formed imposing and elaborate arboreal structures that blocked the view. People walked along a network of twisted paths and blind alleys searching for the way out. Labyrinths were widespread in France, England, and Holland. They were a source of amusement for ladies and their suitors; couples would walk about, weaving plots and relationships. Later, the paths were widened and adorned with decorative plants, sculptures, fountains, and increasingly complicated symbolic representations.

Usually, the middle of a labyrinth contained a stand or a raised tower so that a person who was lost could find the way out. Perhaps the purpose of the tower was also to keep an eye on what was happening within the winding maze. With the

Labyrinths, with their winding paths, blind alleys, and hidden corners, were once the ideal place for romantic encounters. It was in the labyrinth at Woodstock Castle, for example, that Henry II of England used to meet secretly with his beloved Rosamund, far from the eyes of his wife. In the name of public morality, the famous labyrinth of Schönbrunn Castle in Vienna was destroyed.

arrival of the country garden, especially during the early nineteenth century, many labyrinths were destroyed or neglected, although some in public parks survived. With the renewed love of formality and topiary, they reappeared in the second half of the nineteenth century, even in private gardens. In recent times, the great concern for large historical gardens prompted the restoration or reconstruction of several labyrinths, especially in England. For example, the labyrinth in the garden in Hampton Court, one of the oldest, is a national monument today.

Among English labyrinths, the most remarkable are found in Crystal Palace Park, south of London, in Bridge End Garden in Essex, and in Glenduragan in Cornwall.

The garden in Floor Castle in Scotland, the one at Chatsworth Castle near Nottingham, and at the one at Longleat House in Wiltshire are recent creations. Also worth noting are the elaborate Marlborough Maze in Blenheim Palace in Oxfordshire, in whose hedges canons, trumpets, and other shapes are modeled, and the one in Merritown House in Dorset, where various

characters from *Alice in Wonderland* are carved. In Italy, however, few labyrinths have survived. Among them are those at Villa Garzoni in Collodi, Villa Barbarigo in Valsanzibio, Villa Pisani in Strà, Villa Rizzardi in Pojega di Negrar, and Villa Giusti in Verona. Several, such as the last named, are in terrible condition. In France, one of the most unusual is the Labyrinthe Bleu, found in the castle of Noirieux in Briollay, so named because it was

How to Walk Through a Labyrinth

A good labyrinth connects two points through the most winding path possible. In reality, you can travel through any labyrinth without losing your way, because all labyrinths are made according to specific geometric and mathematical rules. In order not to get lost, you must always stay on the same side of the path (right or left) that you are walking on. At each crossroads, you must always take the closest road (taking a left turn if you walk on the left side; a right turn if you are on the right side). If a new path takes you to a crossroads that you have already passed through, or if you reach a dead end, you must turn back to the old path. If the old path takes you to a familiar crossroads or to a dead end, you must take a new one. Only if there is no new one do you go back on the old road.

made of *Ceanothus impressus*, with small, shiny, persistent leaves and extraordinary blue flowers. Although you can find some labyrinths with modern interpretations in public parks and large private gardens, the size of the area needed to create one limits its popularity. In small private gardens, however, you can create a hint of one with partial hedges or blocks in the form of a parallel side hedge, suitably placed, to define the borders of other plants. The traditional plants used for making labyrinths are boxwood, yew, hornbeam, beech, and laurel, but recently hawthorn, cotoneaster, thuja, and juniper have also been used.

Below and at right, details of the labyrinth of the Villa Pisani in Strà, where a small tower allows you to find your way out if you get lost.

Rows of Trees & Garden Paths

Characteristic features of the French-style garden were rows of deciduous trees with interwoven leaves on the top, trained in the shape of candelabra or as a continuous and very long green wall. These require medium or large gardens.

Their function is mainly architectural and structural: they emphasize the main axes and panoramic views, stressing the importance of a pathway and creating a light physical barrier that increases the sense of depth. You can create them with evergreen and deciduous plants. The first are more suitable when you want to create permanent barriers that are massive and impenetrable; the second are subject to the changing seasons and offer lightness and transparency.

The development of the frame of the trees begins on the trunk, $7\frac{1}{2}$ feet (2.5 m) from the ground for the largest species. At this point, you can form the foliage in the candelabra shape, interwoven on the top or trimmed on the sides and left to grow freely on top. With the smaller species, the leaves open at $4\frac{1}{2}$ –$5\frac{1}{2}$ feet (1.5–1.8 m) from the ground. We usually leave these free or weave or train them in the candelabra shape or as a raised hedge. The raised hedge is halfway between a

*I*n Boboli Garden, high evergreen walls of holly enclose a charming path.

row of trees and a hedge. It is made of smaller trees, and the parallel side is shaped on the bare trunks. Begin with plants that are young, but higher than the height where they will be formed. Plant at varying distances of 3–12 feet (1.2–4 m), according to the strength of the species used. Prepare a frame of metal wires on several levels, $1\frac{1}{2}$ –2 feet (50–60 cm) apart from each other, starting from the height set for shaping the foliage. In each plant, remove all the side shoots up to the desired height and bend the others softly and fasten them to the wires of the frame. When the hedge has reached its definitive shape and size, remove the frame and trim the new vegetation regularly. They will require a considerable amount of time to keep them orderly and neat.

*T*o the right, an example of a raised hedge of hornbeam in London's Kew Gardens.

Geometric and Fantastic Green Sculptures

Since the dawn of topiary art, people have modeled plants into innumerable shapes, from the simplest, such as spheres, cones, and pyramids, to the most complex, geometric, fantastic, and animated, including full action scenes, such as the fox hunt with entire packs of dogs.

Today, in the large collections and in small country gardens, you can find shapes of every kind: teapots, giant locomotives, gondolas, elephants, horses rampant, birds, dogs, angels in prayer, crowns, windmills, dinosaurs, and even the Loch Ness monster.

The size, the style of the garden, and the house should determine the number, shape, placement, and function of topiary figures. You can use these shapes to emphasize walkways and paths, enrich a hedge or an arch, adorn the corners of a rectangular flower bed, or highlight a foreshortened view of the surrounding landscape. Suitably placed, green sculptures become irresistible focal points in a geometric flower bed design, a vegetable garden, or a small city garden. They can ornament a door, a portico, or a balcony and lend interest to an anonymous corner. The most elaborate or imaginative figures attract the eye; they create surprise and movement and, if used with discretion, amusement. However, you should stick to simplicity in the design of the garden and in the shape of the plant, so that you don't overdo it and make your garden appear ridiculous. Use imaginative shapes in moderation and position them in spots that are slightly out of the way, or at least not continually in sight. They are particularly suited to be grown in a pot. Thus, they can be moved if necessary, especially if they are made on metal structures, whose unnatural rigidity would somehow seem

The unexpected presence in the garden of a small green dog.

inappropriate in the middle of the garden. The simplest shapes, on the other hand, are a better choice for someone who is new to this art form because they are easier to create. You can always enhance them later, adding shapes to the top, for example, a cube topped off with a semi-circle, an obelisk with a ring, a series of shelves with a cone, a truncated pyramid with a little bird. For the more complex shapes, use a metal structure to train the branches or as a guide in trimming.

*W*ith topiary you can make static figures, but you can also use motion. A nice example of this is "The Fox Hunt," depicted in the United States and England, which shows a pack of dogs pursuing a fox.

Cloud Shapes

Growing evergreen plants, usually conifers, in the shape of a cloud stems from the Oriental bonsai technique. This shape works well for small gardens, balconies, and courtyards, giving any corner a touch of elegance. A wall or a dark hedge provides a striking background, allowing the movement of the branches to stand out.

Use the cloud shape with species whose branch structure is as interesting as the foliage and with plants that you want to grow in the shelter of a wall.

You need to begin with a plant that is already somewhat developed, carefully choosing the initial shape, considering the desired end result and the distribution of the leaves. Be careful because mistakes can require a year or two to correct. Cut off all excess lateral shoots at the base, stripping the branches and leaving only the top foliage, which you will trim in a rounded shape.

Cloud-shaped topiaries, potted or planted in the ground, enhance the decorative characteristics of the bark.

Candelabra-Shaped Trees

In gardens and on tree-lined streets, you can still find maples, plane trees, lindens, and horse chestnut trees trained in the form of candelabra, with rounded leaves and the main branches shaped like large knuckles.

This kind of shaping, besides being very decorative, makes it possible to keep the foliage

small on trees that grow large. However, you need to start with young plants that are easily shaped and have the ability to heal quickly from the trimming. Every year or two, you must cut off the new shoots. This way, the surface of the cut will always be small and easy to heal.

Don't confuse growing a tree in the shape of a candelabra with pollarding. This practice, in which the leaves of an adult tree are drastically reduced by cropping the large branches, has been condemned. Besides destroying the natural development of the plant, pollarding weakens it because the effort expended in healing the large wounds makes it susceptible to disease and pests.

These trees are trained in the candelabra shape.

Interweavings, Arcades, and Green Niches

The custom of making arcades, pergolas, and niches by weaving together the foliage of trees and shrubs with strong but flexible branches, such as the linden tree, hornbeam, laburnum, and fruit-bearing plants, hails back to ancient Rome. These charming weavings of greenery were just as fashionable in the enclosed gardens of the sixteenth century as they were in the Roman era. They have once again become popular, especially for small gardens. They divide the space and create hidden passageways and dark corners that lend the garden variety, intimacy, and atmosphere.

You should start with young plants, approximately two years of age. Depending on the species and the result you wish to obtain, plant them at spaced intervals of $2\frac{1}{2}$ –$3\frac{1}{2}$ feet (0.8–1.2 m) to 12–15 feet (4–5 m) apart on both sides of a path. To create niches, plant them along a curved line. Approximately 4–8 inches (10–20 cm)

An arcade of laburnum in Kew Gardens in London made with a metal structure.

behind each plant, place a guide, fastening it to the trunk with raffia or cord. Depending on whether you want an arcade, a niche, or a pergola, prepare the appropriate wooden or metal frame. For a pergola, the plants are left to grow until the trunks reach $6–7\frac{1}{2}$ feet (2–2.5 m) in height. Then, before the plants renew themselves, the tops are cut off, forcing the plants to sprout many lateral leaves. In the summer, cut all the new leaves at the base, leaving only three or four tied to the supporting structure. Every year at the end of winter, trim one-third of the branches that are part of the set shape and remove all the new shoots that are not. To create an arcade, let the plants grow to the height where you want the curve to begin. Remove all the shoots that grow in the opposite direction of the curvature and train the remaining ones along the frame until you have created a complete arch of branches.

Treillage, Trellis, and Two-Dimensional Green Sculpture

You can train shrubs and climbers to take on a desired shape by leaning them against lattices, trellises, or tripods. During the nineteenth century, the latter were often used for growing roses decorated with hearts, garlands, or other decorations on the top. Today, we use them for many other climbers and for vegetable gardens. With wooden or bamboo trellises and treillage, you can make espaliers and two-dimensional green sculptures that are just right for small spaces and balconies. As cordons, festoons, signs, various abstract ornamental motifs, and geometric or imaginary figures, you can force them to grow flat against a wall, perhaps on a door frame or a window. Often, treillages are created in such a way as to deceive the eye and give the illusion of depth where there is none. The ancient Romans used this technique.

At right, a pear tree arcade in which the frame was removed when the curve was finished.

Espaliers

Apple trees, pear trees, apricot trees, *Ceanothus*, camellias, cherry trees, *Pyracantha*, magnolias, and many other trees and shrubs lend themselves to being trained as espaliers. In the ground or in pots, they are extremely decorative. They can also be grown in very small gardens and on balconies.

The term "espalier" refers to plants trained to grow two-dimensionally, usually against a wall, according to a traditional geometric design: in the shape of a U, a double U, a cordon, a candelabrum, a Y, a fan, or in more elaborate shapes. Because they are not three-dimensional and because they are trimmed to maintain a shape, the plants occupy little space. Any one of a variety of fruit trees with limited development, grafted on dwarf stock, will require even less space. The custom of raising fruit plants in a set shape dates at least as far back as the ancient Romans. However, since the fifteenth century, the two-dimensional form has been particularly popular. It was nearly an obsession in nineteenth-century gardens. Besides giving the plants a formal, ordered appearance, the presence of a wall that absorbs and releases heat protects the plants from wind and frosts.

A raised hornbeam espalier.

Espaliers are extremely decorative: an uninteresting wall, a door, a shed, or the space between two windows can be beautified, framed by a fig tree, a fragrant laburnum, or a fiery pyracantha. You can enhance the charm of a vegetable garden enclosed by a wall, a well-exposed balcony, or a courtyard with a few small apple trees, a light blue *Ceanothus*, a flowering cherry tree, or a camellia. Today "high" espaliers are very common, made up of a row of deciduous trees, such as linden, beech, and hornbeam. They should not lean directly against a wall. Instead, they should rest against an iron wire structure, and the branches should be trained to grow horizontally, evenly spaced, to make a flat structure of six or seven levels that begins at a certain height from the ground.

At right, growing fruit trees and some shrubs into espaliers highlights their ornamental nature.

Espaliers

Traditionally, apple and pear trees are the fruit trees most commonly trained as espaliers. However, it is not unusual to see apricot, plum, peach, cherry, fig, citrus, olive trees, *Magnolia grandiflora*, *Pyracantha*, and *Ceanothus* trained against a wall.

Espaliers can be made in a variety of ways, from simple to very elaborate.

*F*an-shaped espalier: *Similar to a palmette espalier, but the branches are inserted obliquely, just above ground level.*

*P*almette espalier: *From the trunk, at a certain height from the ground, several pairs of oblique branches grow on opposite sides. In a variation of this, called the "Y palmette," there are two primary branches, while in the "free palmette" the branches are inserted irregularly along the trunk.*

*C*andelabra espalier: *Also called the "forked cordon" espalier and the "Verrier palmette" espalier, this espalier is made of several superimposed levels, each in the shape of a U.*

*D*ouble U espalier: *Each primary branch opens up into a curve, forming a U.*

Double cordon espalier: The cordons are made of horizontal branches that have small, very short branches, called "spurs," growing on them. The trunk can be vertical or slanted (45-degree angle) with one branch or two facing branches.

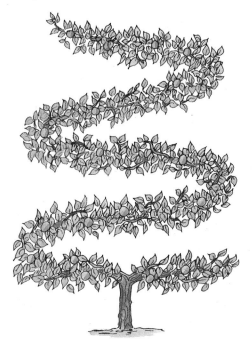

Zigzag cordon espalier: The trunk winds in a curving progression. This shape is very rare today because it is difficult to create.

Arched espalier: This form is also rather rare today. It consists of a bilateral cordon on several levels. Horizontal branches and fruit-bearing branches are arched for the highest fruit yield.

Curved fan espalier: This is a variation of the fan espalier. It is another form that we rarely find today. Here, the lateral branches are slanted and alternate on a trunk that grows in a zigzag.

U-shaped espalier: Approximately 1½ feet (50 cm) off the ground, the vertical trunk opens up into two branches. These move horizontally and then vertically.

Hedges and Sculptures with Ivy

Ivy is a hardy climber that grows well in the sun and in the shade. You can use it in many ways: to create two-dimensional designs on a wall, to cover up metal structures, and to create hedges.

To create two-dimensional designs on a wall, begin with young plants or with ivy that is already developed and clinging to the wall. If you are using ivy that is already there, you may need to remove and cut some of the older branches in order to create the desired design. This may leave a trace on the supporting wall that is difficult to remove.

If you start with young plants, the work is simpler. Before placing them in their permanent spots, sketch the outline of the design on the wall, using a rope and some nails. This will give you a good idea of the general effect and the proportions. You can make corrections before proceeding.

At the beginning of spring, crop the old leaves to form a flat design and to stimulate the growth of abundant new vegetation that you will train according to the set design. You may have to intervene two or three times during spring to control the development.

Use young ivy plants to cover the structures, selecting varieties with small, light leaves. Trim the tops a few times to stimulate a dense and abundant growth that will hide the frame. After that, a light trimming from time to time is sufficient to maintain a neat appearance.

To make a hedge that is 3–3½ feet (1–1.2 m) high, you need to use large-leaf ivy (*Hedera helix*). No support is needed; in fact, with time, it tends to take on a shrub-like bearing.

Arrange the seedlings in two staggered rows, 12–15 inches (30–40 cm) apart. As they grow, trim the branches so that they don't expand in width. When the plants have assumed a shrubby bearing and the desired height, you need to clip the new shoots only once or twice a year during the summer.

At left, the color contrast produced by different varieties of ivy trained on a metal frame.

At right, evergreen and slow-growing ivy can neatly decorate walls and façades.

Simple and composite geometric shapes

Topiary shapes taken from ancient gardens

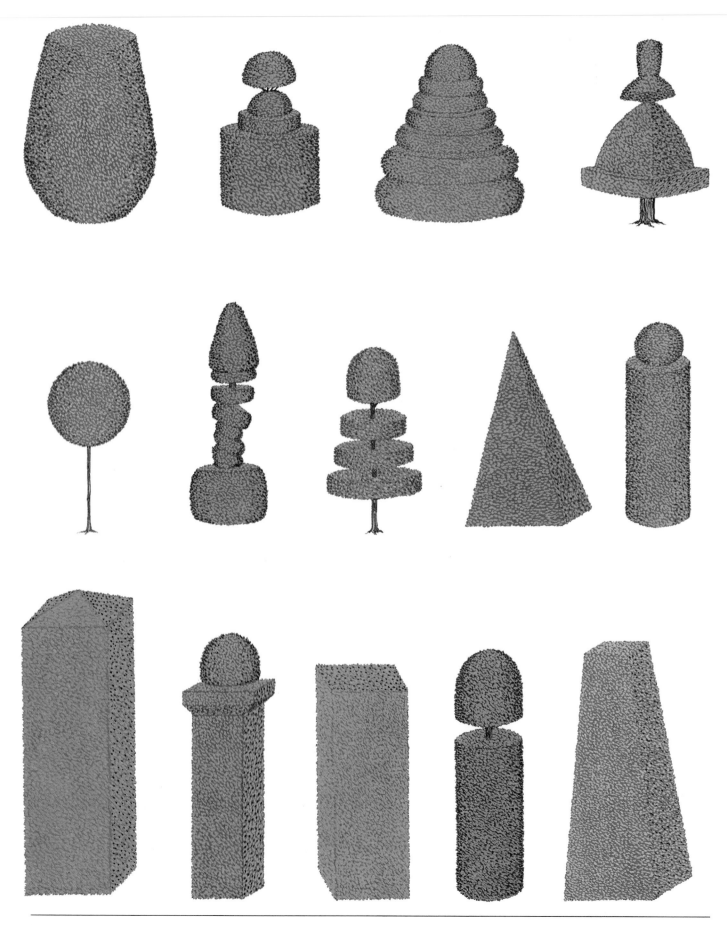

The Plants

Many trees and shrubs, deciduous or evergreen, lend themselves to certain shapes. Their bearing, ability to respond to frequent pruning, size, and the characteristics of their foliage make them more or less suited for hedges, rows of trees, or for geometric or imaginative shapes.

The Plants

Some plants, such as yew, boxwood, ilex, and myrtle, are traditional plants found in the oldest paintings and referred to in the oldest texts. Evergreens and plants of Mediterranean origin connect Arab gardens to Roman gardens and the gardens of the Old World to American gardens in a continuous evolutionary path over the centuries.

Many plants were introduced in Europe after topiary's difficult period, between the fifteenth and seventeenth centuries. Magnolias and tsugas, for example, entered topiary only in the eighteenth century; camellias around the end of the seventeenth; laburnum, though cultivated for about five hundred years, was only used for pergolas at the end of the nineteenth century. The practice of molding fruit trees and shrubs into unnatural shapes such as espaliers, fans, and cordons is very old. The custom of making green sculptures and training shrubs, such as myrtle, or climbers, such as ivy and jasmine, on iron or wood supports is rather old. At the end of the sixteenth century, G.V. Soderini wrote in *Della coltura degli orti e dei giardini:* "With scissors you can make the shapes asked of you—animals, ships, galleys, vases, needle-fish, balls, squares, fortifications, towers, houses, and palaces—having first formed all these things with iron wire

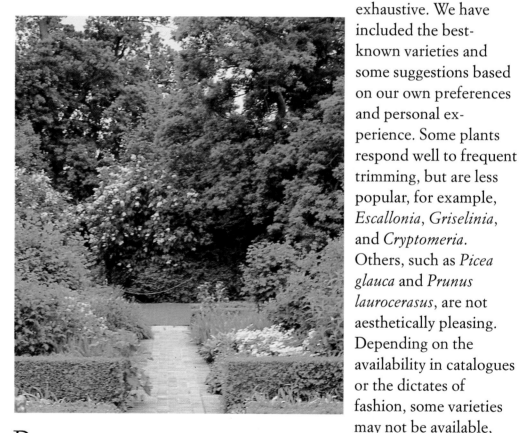

*D*warf boxwood hedges give structure and life to the flower beds.

and then following this model and covering it with twigs." The list of species and varieties is not exhaustive. We have included the best-known varieties and some suggestions based on our own preferences and personal experience. Some plants respond well to frequent trimming, but are less popular, for example, *Escallonia*, *Griselinia*, and *Cryptomeria*. Others, such as *Picea glauca* and *Prunus laurocerasus*, are not aesthetically pleasing. Depending on the availability in catalogues or the dictates of fashion, some varieties may not be available, while others, which are equally good, may be. The information gathered in this book is a basis for venturing onto new roads. Remember that the shaping should be geared to support and highlight the characteristics of the chosen plants.

*A*t right, the Villa Lante della Rovere, in Bagnaia, is a good example of the juxtaposition of boxwood and yew in a sixteenth-century design.

Deciduous Trees, Small Trees, and Shrubs

A majority of the plants used in topiary are evergreen because they keep their leaves year round; thus, their architectural value remains unchanged. In reality, deciduous plants lend themselves just as well to the creation of green sculptures.

In fact, deciduous plants have several advantages. They withstand pollution better because every fall, as they shed their leaves, they also shed all of the toxic substances that have accumulated in them. They can be trimmed with power hedge cutters instead of shears and, therefore, with greater speed. In addition, leaves that are cut in half during the trimming process do not stay on the plant for very long, as can happen with evergreen leaves.

Finally, bare trees and shrubs possess a certain special beauty; in fact, it is in the winter that the true essence of these plants is revealed.

Among the listed species, some are more suited to making rows of tree or large hedges, others to arches or pergolas (using the technique called "pleaching"), others still to standards, and others to geometric shapes.

Barberry
(*Berberidaceae: Berberis calliantha, B.* x *ottawensis, B.* x *stenophyllia, B. thunbergii, B. wilsoniae*) The deciduous Barberry deserves to be more popular than it is. These compact and orderly shrubs, which are more or less thorny, make very decorative hedges 3–5 feet (1–1.5 m) high. In the fall, bunches of red or yellow berries that follow small yellow or yellow-orange flowers shine through the warm tones of the small leaves. These plants can be cultivated in any soil that it is not too moist and is in full sun.

The best known is *B. thunbergii* ('Atropurpurea', Zones 5–8), whose red-brown and purple foliage is very difficult to place near other plants. Naturally dense and compact, these plants need pruning in late winter and, if necessary, also at the end of summer.

European Beech
(*Fagaceae: Fagus sylvatica*, Zones 5–7) This tree has splendid foliage, soft green in spring, then darker and glossy, and finally a warm yellow brown. Most of the leaves of the hedge remain on the plant for nearly the entire winter. The tree is suited to any kind of earth, even alkaline soil, provided that it is not too heavy. It can tolerate shade. The hedges grow 8–10 feet (2.5–3 m) high; rows of trees grow 26–32 feet (8–10 m) tall. Prune the beech in June and late summer. This late-summer pruning ensures that the young leaves remain on the branches well into winter.

Sometimes it is necessary to trim again during the plant's dormant period.

European Hornbeam
(*Betulaceae: Carpinus betulus, C.b.* 'Fastigiata', Zones 5–8) The leaves are a soft green yellow when newly sprouted, but they become darker at maturity and turn yellow brown in the fall. They remain on the plant for a long time during the winter. The hornbeam is one of the most versatile plants. It thrives in rich, fertile soil, but also in soil that has a lot of clay and in alkaline soil, in sun or in full shade. It can be cut and shaped into large hedges 6–10 feet (2–3 m) tall and higher, arches, standards, pergolas, bird snares, niches, arcades, and rows of trees reaching 19–26 feet (6–8 m) in height. In fact, during the eighteenth century, the hornbeam and the elm were typically used to make green arcades that ran along the outer borders of the garden or uncoiled in winding curves.

The variety 'Fastigiata' requires few trimmings because it keeps a wide, pyramidal shape naturally. The *C.b.* 'Monumentalis' is very slow growing and does not require any pruning at all because it naturally maintains a neat and tapered shape. Trim it in June and late summer.

European Horse Chestnut
(*Hippocastanaceae: Aesculus hippocastanum*, Zones 4–7) The size of the leaves and the way they are laid out on the branches prevent this large tree from being used for large geometric espaliers the way you use the hedge maple, hornbeam, and beech. However, you can grow it in a set shape because it withstands frequent and severe pruning. The umbrella, for example, is a classic shape. The branch structure begins approximately 8 feet (2.5 m) from the ground. The horse chestnut is suited to most soils and tolerates partial shade, but if it will be exposed to full sun, avoid placing it in a paved area because the heat reflected from the pavement can scorch the leaves. Prune it at the end of the plant's winter dormant period.

*T*he intimacy of a secret garden created with high hedges, even if deciduous, remains unchanged in winter.

Hawthorn

(*Rosaceae*: *Crataegus monogyna, C. laevigatia,* Zones 5–7) Hawthorns are large shrubs or small trees that reach 13–26 feet (4–8 m) in height. Plants for free-form and formal hedges range from 6–19 feet (2–6 m) high. Hawthorns thrive in any kind of soil, even soil with a lot of clay, but they need full sun. Compact and thorny, they grow rather quickly two to three years after you plant them in the garden. They withstand any kind of trimming, and even if grown free-form, they are rich in flowers and very decorative red fruit. When trimmed to make a formal hedge, they lose a part of the floriferous branches. If you must reshape a neglected hedge, you should prune before plant renewal, shortening the branches which developed in the previous year by at least one-half to two-thirds. In general, you should trim in June and repeat the cutting in August.

Hedge Maple

(*Aceraceae*: *Acer campestre,* Zones 5–8) The hedge maple is a very interesting tree because of its beautifully shaped, smooth and glossy, dark green leaves. In the fall, these change to warm golden tones. The plant is commonly found in European wild hedges in soil that has a lot of clay or is alkaline. It grows well in full sun or in part shade.

Because it does not have a very rapid growth rate, it lends itself to making compact, orderly hedges, 6–26 feet (2–8 m) tall or higher. The rows of trees at Schönbrunn Castle are famous, reaching 32 feet (10 m) in height.

Maples and other deciduous plants were typically found in the French gardens of the eighteenth century. They were grown in paths *en rivière*: the plants were cut along the sides, but left to grow freely skyward in the high part of the foliage, forming a frame of leaves.

The hedge maple is pruned once or twice in June and in late summer. It may also be pruned at the end of winter if the hedge needs to be renewed.

Linden

(*Tiliaceae*: *Tilia* sp., Zones 4–7) The linden is a very versatile large tree. You can use it for large tree-lined hedges more that 13 feet (4 m) high, and you can also grow it in an umbrella shape the way you would a horse chestnut or plane tree. It tolerates any type of soil, but prefers rich, deep soils that are slightly damp, in full sun. The species *T. x euchlora* is the least prone to aphid attacks and the production of honeydew. Place other species far from areas that are heavily trafficked. The linden stands up well to trimming, which should be accomplished during the plant's dormant period.

Plane Tree

(*Platanaceae*: *Platanus* sp., Zones 5–9) The plane tree is large with beautiful bark speckled with shades of cream and green. It is frequently used in rows of trees to line streets. As is the case with the horse chestnut or linden, you can grow it in the classic candelabra shape, the branch structure starting no less than 8 feet (2.5 m) from the ground. It stands up well even to drastic trimmings. In the European countryside, it was used to divide the fields and was cut periodically at the base. It prefers full sun and soil that is deep, cool, and not too alkaline. Prune it during the plant's winter dormant period. The emperor Caligula was said to have a giant plane tree in his garden. It was trimmed so that the upper branches formed stands and the lower ones formed steps on which up to fifteen people could sit comfortably to eat around a table.

Privet

(*Oleaceae*: *Ligustrum ovalifolium,* Zones 6–8; *L. x vicaryi,* Zones 5–8) Privet is a semi-evergreen or deciduous shrub that, depending on the severity of the winter temperature, loses or keeps part of its small and glossy dark green leaves. It is suited to any type of soil as long as it is in full sun, where it grows very quickly. You can easily attach the flexible branches to metal structures of various shapes. When grown as a hedge, you must trim it frequently for the first few years so that it forms compact branches at the base. Often scorned because people consider it too unassuming or common, privet grows compactly and with its tiny foliage makes very decorative country hedges. Trim it often, at least three to five times between the beginning and end of summer.

A hornbeam hedge is decorative in the winter because of the close weaving of its bare branches.

At right, evergreens grown in topiary shapes enhance deciduous plants.

Broadleaf Evergreen Trees and Shrubs

Holly

(*Aquifoliaceae*: *Ilex* sp., Zones
5–9) Holly makes an impenetrable
hedge 5–13 feet (1.5–4 m) high. You
can grow it in many geometric
shapes in the ground and in pots.
The elegant glossy foliage,
dark green or variegated with
white and yellow, is leathery, thorny, and very
dense. Holly makes a splendid hedge, an
excellent background for herbaceous or shrubby
blossoms. It is suited to any type of soil, even dry
and lightly alkaline, but prefers rich, fertile soil
in full sun as well as in deep shade. Prune it
once or twice a season: at the beginning
of spring and, if necessary, at the end of
summer. The initial cost of the
planting is higher than other more
popular and faster-growing
evergreen hedge plants, but after
the first three or four years, holly
needs little upkeep and is not prone
to any disease.

A holly hedge can provoke
outrageous behavior. According to the story,
during a stay in England, Czar Peter the Great took
lodgings in an estate where a splendid hedge of holly
thrived. As a pastime, the monarch sat in a wheelbarrow
and had himself pushed against the hedge. Shortly
thereafter, he was thrown out by the owner of the house
who, like all Englishmen, was very fond of his
plants.

Bay, Bay Laurel

(*Lauraceae*: *Laurus nobilis*,
Zones 8–10) A
small tree or
large shrub, the
laurel is (with the yew,
boxwood, and holly) the plant
par excellence of topiary art. It
can be used to make hedges 5–16 feet
(1.5–5 m) high and to create isolated
topiaries. It also grows very well in
containers, but we often grow it in the shape of
a standard, pyramid, or sphere. Its elegant foliage is
dense, mid-sized, glossy, and dark green on the top
of the blade and slightly lighter on its underside. The
laurel's beauty lies in the juxtaposition of these two
different shades of green. Together, they suggest sobriety
and lightness. Its ideal soil is cool and rich in humus, but it
grows well in other types of soil and in different exposures,
from full sun to shade. However, in overly strong shade, it
tends to grow less densely. As a Mediterranean plant, it
does not withstand prolonged periods of intense cold,
especially if the growth is not mature. In regions with
harsh winters, place it in protected locations. Trim it once
or twice a year: the first time at the beginning of spring and
then late in summer.

Barberry

(*Berberidaceaeis*: *Berberis* x *mentorensis*, *B. darwinii*, *B.
julianae*, *B. verrucolosa*, Zones 5–7) The evergreen
Barberry is a thorny shrub that deserves to be more
popular because it is beautiful, versatile, and responsive to
pruning. The plants are suited to protective hedges 3–6
feet (1–2 m) high. You can also grow them as isolated
topiaries to be trimmed into geometric shapes. Their lovely
dark green, glossy, and leathery little leaves are somewhat
like the leaves of the holly. Trimming robs them of part of
their beautiful rich blooms and small blue, yellow, red, or
orange fruit. Although barberry grows much faster than

boxwood and holly, like them it thrives in strong shade. It is suited to any type of soil, does well in full sun, and withstands harsh winter temperatures. Trim it after it blossoms and, if need be, at the end of summer.

Camellia

(*Ericacee*: *Camellia japonica* 'Hagoromo' ['Magnoliaeflora'], *C. maliflora*, *C. sasanqua*, *C.s.* 'Yuletide', Zones 7–9) Camellias are large shrubs suited to splendid espaliers, flowering hedges 5–13 feet (1.5–4 m) high, and isolated topiaries in simple geometric shapes, such as the standard, cone, or pyramid. The leathery, shining leaves of dark green enhance the flowers. Some varieties are more suited than others for green sculptures because they have a naturally compact bearing and small leaves. Camellias grow well only in acid soil that is cool and well drained, in full sun or light shade, in the ground or potted, preferably in areas with a humid climate. Fine examples of topiary hedges are found in large gardens in Portugal, cooled by the humid ocean air. Much hardier than is commonly believed, these plants can tolerate temperatures of about 22° F (–5° C) for short periods. Camellias stand up to pruning, which should occur immediately after the blossoming period. Shorten the vegetation that developed over the preceding year by one-half to two-thirds. You can repeat the trimming during the course of the summer if you want to keep the contours perfectly defined.

Strawberry Tree

(*Ericaceae*: *Arbutus unedo*, *A.u.* 'Compacta', Zones 7–9) The strawberry tree is a naturally compact small tree or large shrub, useful for making espaliers or hedges that are 6–13 feet (2–4 m) high. You can also grow them in geometric shapes, usually in the classic standard shape. The cultivar 'Compacta' grows more slowly and is suitable for small formal hedges no higher that 5 feet (1.5 m) tall. It is one of the most beautiful native Mediterranean plants, particularly

decorative in the fall and winter when white flowers and small red fruit appear together between the bright dark green of the top of the blade and the lighter green of the underside. It grows well in full sun or in shade, preferably in soil rich in humus, but it also tolerates lightly alkaline soil. Somewhat hardy, it can withstand temperatures of approximately 22° F (–5° C) for short periods and, like the laurel, it is able to revegetate from its base if it is damaged. In early spring, prune one-third to one-half of the vegetation of the preceding year.

Cotoneaster

(*Rosaceae*: *Cotoneaster microphyllus*, *C. franchetii*, *C. lacteus*, *C. salicifolius*, Zones 6–8) An evergreen or semi-evergreen shrub, cotoneaster is suited for hedges and espaliers 6–13 feet (2–4 m) high and for green sculptures. Very ornamental in spring and summer with its numerous small white or pinkish flowers, it is also decorative during the fall and much of the winter because of the orange or red fruit. The foliage is tiny, leathery, and bright green, often with a silvery underside. Cotoneaster is useful because of its hardy nature and adaptability to any kind of soil, as long as it is in full sun. Prune it at the end of the blossoming and, if necessary, once again in late summer.

Elaeagnus

(*Elaeagnaceae*: *Elaeagnus* x *ebbingei*, *E. pungens*, Zones 7–9) Elaeagnus is a very rapidly growing large shrub used for hedges 6–13 feet (2–4 m) high, particularly in windy areas and in areas near the sea. It has mid-sized leaves that are silvery or green on the top of the blade and silvery on the underside. The flowers, which are not that striking, are very fragrant and open in the fall, followed by small orange or red fruit that ripens the following spring. The plant thrives in full sun in any type of soil, as long as it is not too alkaline. To make an orderly hedge or a compact windbreak espalier, prune frequently in early spring and again at the beginning of summer.

Japanese Euonymus

(*Celastraceae*: *Euonymus japonicus*, *E.j.* 'Albomarginatus', *E.j.* 'Aureopictus', *E.j.* 'Microphyllus', *E.j.* 'Ovatus Aureus', Zones 7–9) Euonymus is a medium-sized shrub that can be grown in the most simple geometric shapes, such as the cone or the sphere, and in hedges 3–6 feet (1–2 m) high. The medium-sized leaves are glossy and dark green in the typical species and variegated with white or yellow gold in the countless varieties. The different leaf colorings can be used to create color contrasts without having to resort to the use of flowers. The euonymus is a hardy and undemanding plant. It can grow in all soils, rich in humus or sandy, or even slightly alkaline. It is suited to any exposure; however, the variegated types tend to form inner branches with green leaves. It grows well by the sea or in polluted city areas. Because it is prone to attacks of scale, use preventative treatment measures. Trim at the beginning of spring (March–April) and at the end of summer.

Phillyrea

(*Oleaceae*: *Phillyrea angustifolia*, *P. decora*, Zones 8–10) The phillyrea, which deserves to be more popular than it is, is a Mediterranean shrub with a solid, distinct appearance. It is naturally compact and elegant, and it grows rather quickly. The plant is suited for geometric sculptures, especially rounded shapes, with or without structures, and for hedges 4–10 feet (1.2–3 m) high. It has elongated, leathery leaves that are dark and glossy green on top and lighter and dull underneath. The flowers are insignificant, and the fruit is small and blue black. Phillyrea grows in all types of soil, including sandy, in full sun or shade, and even near the sea. It is very hardy and tolerates pruning, which is done at the beginning of spring (March–April) and again at the end of summer or immediately after the flowering.

Live Oak

(*Fagaceae*: *Quercus virginiana*, Zones 7–10) The live oak is a large tree. It is the American equivalent of the European holm oak, traditionally used in Mediterranean regions for green sculptures because of its moderate speed of growth.

The live oak is very decorative and versatile. If you preserve all the branches that start from the ground, it will grow as a large bush, reaching heights of 10–30 feet (3–9 m). If you remove the lower branches, it develops into a large tree, and the thick foliage can be recut in geometric shapes. The leaves are medium-sized, leathery, varying in shape, more or less thorny, dark and glossy green on the top surface of the blade. On the underside they are dull, tomentose, and silvery. Live oak is suited to any soil, even sandy or alkaline, and can grow at the seashore as well as inland. It is a hardier species than commonly believed. In areas with colder winter climates it becomes semideciduous or even fully deciduous. Trim at the beginning of spring and, if necessary, at the end of summer.

Privet

(*Oleaceae*: *Ligustrum japonicum*, *L. ionandrum*, *L. lucidum*, Zones 7–10) Privets are large shrubs or small trees that can be grown in classic and very large geometric shapes or as hedges 6–19 feet (2–6 m) high. Because of the small leaves and the flexibility of the branches, privets are often used to create small green sculptures in the shape of animals, jugs, hearts, helicopters, baskets, etc. In fact, the possibilities are endless for the imaginative, enthusiastic gardener.

The leaves are leathery, dark green, glossy, and large, with the exception of the *L. ionandrum* (*L. delavayanum*), which has medium-sized leaves and is used for small topiaries. Privet is suited to any kind of soil as long as it is in full sun. Privets with very large leaves are not completely hardy, even if they can revegetate quickly when damaged by the cold. When grown as hedges, they should usually be pruned twice: at the beginning of spring and again at the end of summer, but much more frequently (up to four to six times) when used for green sculptures.

Honeysuckle

(*Caprifoliaceae*: *Lonicera nitida*, *L.n.* 'Baggesen's Gold', *L. pileata*, Zones 7–9) Honeysuckle is a shrub that is useful for borders or hedges 3–6 feet (1–2 m) high. It grows quickly and withstands pruning well. The tiny leaves are glossy dark or golden green. It is not one of the best shrubs for topiaries because of its somewhat disorderly bearing. It needs frequent pruning to maintain its compactness. Instead, because of the flexibility of its branches, honeysuckle is ideal for making green sculptures using metal structures. The smaller *L. pileata* naturally keeps an even shape, with branches parallel to the ground. Honeysuckle grows in any soil, even near the sea, in the sun or in strong shade. Trim it two or three times during the summer.

Southern Magnolia

(*Magnoliaceae*: *Magnolia grandiflora*, Zones 7–9) The magnolia is a large tree which you can grow as a separate entity, use to make rows of trees, or train as an espalier up to 13–30 feet (4–9 m) high. The very large flowers are extremely fragrant. The magnificent leaves are leathery and glossy on the top of the blade. The underside is dull, tomentose, and brownish. These trees grow in cool, acid soil that is rich in humus, in full sun. In areas with very harsh winter climates, they will grow as espaliers or in bushes, up against a wall that is shaded until midday. Southern magnolias withstand trimmings well and grow slowly. Prune once a year in spring to preserve the compact, orderly shape.

Myrtle

(*Myrtaceae*: *Myrtus communis* and varieties, *Myrtus c. tarentina*, *Myrtus apiculata*, *Myrtus luma*, *Myrtus ugni*, Zones 9–10) An elegant shrub characteristic of the Mediterranean maquis, the myrtle has beautiful dark green, leathery, glossy leaves. During the summer it is covered in small white flowers; in fall, in blue, mahogany, or white berries that are not lost with trimming. Sacred to Venus, the Goddess of Love, it was cultivated by the Romans. According to Virgil in his *Bucolics*, "And you, laurels, I will gather and you, too; myrtle, who is by their side, because placed in this way, your delicate fragrances will be mingled." Horace also speaks of this "very pleasing…beautiful Venus' myrtle." Myrtle continues to be used for small borders 3–6 feet (1–2 m) high or for isolated topiaries 6–10 feet (2–3 m) high. For the most part, myrtle is trimmed in a spherical or semispherical shape. Because its thin branches are very flexible, you can easily train it on structures, making varied green sculptures.

It is not completely hardy, but if the wood is ripened, it can withstand temperatures of 32° F (2–3° C). It is, therefore, suited to gardens by the sea and on the shore of lakes. Myrtle prefers full sun and slightly acidic, as well as slightly alkaline, soil. Trim at the beginning of spring and, if needed to keep its shape, during the summer. It also withstands drastic rejuvenation trimmings well. Do these at the beginning of the vegetative season.

Olearia—Daisy Bush

(*Compositae*: *Olearia* x *hastii*, *O. nummularifolia*, *O.* x *scilloniensis*, *O. solandri*, *O. traversii*, *O.* 'Waikariensis', Zones 8–10) Olearia is a shrub of varying size, leaf shape, and hardiness. Due to its naturally compact bearing and its ability to withstand pruning, it lends itself to the creation

THE PLANTS

of borders 2–2½ feet (60–80 cm) tall, hedges 3–10 feet (1–3 m) tall (*O.* x *scilloniensis* and *O. traversii*) and to isolated topiaries with rounded contours. It has lovely light leaves, sage green or gray green, that are often tomentose and silvery underneath. Olearia grows in sandy or alkaline soil that is loose and well drained, in full sun, and also by the sea. *O.* x *hastii* and *O. nummularifolia* are the hardiest species; the others are only suited to climates with mild winters. Trim for reshaping and rejuvenation at the beginning of spring. Another cutting may be necessary immediately after the summer bloom.

Osmanthus—False Holly, Sweet Holly

(*Oleaceae*: *Osmanthus fragrans*, *O.f.* 'Aurantiacus', *O.* x *fortunei*, *O. delavayi*, *O. heterophyllus*, Zones 7–9) Osmanthus has very fragrant, small, white flowers. The leaves are glossy, leathery, dark green, and of differing size, depending on the species. *Osmanthus delavayi* has olive-green leaves which are small, like boxwood leaves, and thin, flexible branches. It is well suited to make sculptures on structures, hedges, and espaliers 3–5 feet (1–1.5 m) tall, but it is rather slow growing and needs frequent pruning to stay compact. *O. fragrans*, naturally compact and neat, is one of the most beautiful and elegant evergreens. It is particularly noteworthy for the exquisite fragrance given off by its tiny flowers in May and September. Suited to wonderful hedges 6–13 feet (2–4 m) tall and to rounded green sculptures, it is not entirely hardy. In regions with harsh winters, it must be grown as a bush against a wall. *O. heterophyllus*, with leaves similar to those of holly, grows very quickly and requires frequent summer pruning. It is ideal for hedges 10–15 feet (3–5 m) tall and for large green sculptures. Due to its fast growth rate and adaptability, it should be more popular, for example, than the cherry laurel. Osmanthus can be grown in any soil, in full sun or in part shade. Prune at the beginning of spring (March–April) and, if necessary, repeat once or twice during the summer.

Osmarea

(*Oleaceae*: x *Osmarea* 'Burkwoodii', also *Osmanthus* x *bushwoodii*, Zones 6–9) Osmarea is a slow-growing shrub with fragrant flowers and small, leathery, dark green leaves which are glossy on the top. The plant is suited to simple geometric green sculptures, free-form or using a metal structure, and for formal hedges 4–8 feet (1.2–2.5 m) tall. Osmarea is very hardy and withstands trimming well. It grows in full sun, in any soil, even in alkaline soil and soil that is not very deep. Trim after the flowering period, in May or June.

Pittosporum

(*Pittosporaceae*: *Pittosporum crassifolium*, *P. heterophyllum*, *P. phillyraeioides*, *P. ralphii*, *P. tenuifolium*, *P. tobira*, *P.t.* 'Nanum', *P.t.* 'Variegatum', Zones 8–10) Pittosporum is a very ornamental large shrub or small tree with lovely glossy foliage, dark green, olive green, or cream-colored variegations, and numerous fragrant white or purple flowers. In coastal areas, it is indispensable for creating hedges 2½–5 feet (0.75–1.5 m) tall because it withstands sea breezes very well. You can also create espaliers or green sculptures using the interesting fast-growing varieties of the rather monotonous but very popular *Pittosporum tobira*. The dwarf variety of *P. tobira*, because of its compact and round shape, can be considered a natural green sculpture. Pittosporum grows in all types of soil, even alkaline or sandy, in full sun or light shade; it withstands temperatures of 30° F (–1° C) for short periods, especially if the wood has ripened. If the top is damaged by frost, the plant will revegetate with ease after you prune it in spring (March–April). Also prune it once or twice during the summer.

Pyracantha—Firethorn

(*Rosaceae*: *Pyracantha angustifolia*, *P. coccinea*, Zones 6–9) Pyracanthas are large shrubs that can be grown as espaliers. They are unequaled for creating large, impenetrable hedges 6–13 feet (2–4 m) high. They have intense, bright green leaves that are medium small. At the beginning of the summer, the plants are covered with bunches of small white flowers. These are followed by spectacular orange, yellow, or scarlet berries that stay on the plant from September to March. Quick-growing, very hardy, and able to survive pollution, they are suited to all soils, even heavy or alkaline, in full sun. After they bloom, they withstand drastic maintenance prunings in summer.

Portugual Laurel, Cherry Laurel

(*Rosaceae*: *Prunus lusitanica*, Zones 7–8; *P. laurocerasus* 'Otto Luyken', *P.l.* 'Schipkaensis', *P.l.* 'Herbergii', Zones 6–8) These evergreens are small trees or large and medium shrubs with long, leathery, glossy, rather large, elegant leaves. Excellent plants for hedges, in shade or full sun, they withstand wind well. Depending on the variety, you can create hedges 5–10 feet (1.5–3 m) high with *P. lusitanica* and *P. laurocerasus* 'Herbergii' and 'Schipkaensis' and hedges 3–5 feet (0.9–1.5m) high with *P. laurocerasus* 'Otto Luyken' always at least 2 feet (0.6 m) thick. The *P. lusitanica* can also be trained into a standard and can replace the laurel in areas where the latter would be too delicate.

Highly adaptable plants, they grow in any soil that is not excessively alkaline. They withstand drastic pruning, but avoid using hedge trimmers, because you will cut off part of the very large leaves. These will stay on the plant, spoiling the appearance. Instead, use shears at the end of August, or the end of winter in case the hedge needs to be rejuvenated.

Groundsel Bush

(*Compositae*: *Senecio maritima*, 'Dusty Miller', Zones 9–10; *S. monroi*, *S.* 'Sunshine') A typical Mediterranean shrub, very resistant to heat and dry weather, groundsel has oval, gray-green, tomentose leaves. It makes low hedges and borders with a semicircular outline of 2–3 feet (0.8–1 m). It grows in any type of soil that is not too damp, and in full sun. It does well by the sea. Trim at the beginning of spring in order to develop thick, rich foliage; rejuvenate by cutting the old branches at ground level.

Teucrium—Tree Germander

(*Labiatae*: *Teucrium fruticans*, Zones 8–10) An aromatic shrub, typical of the Mediterranean maquis, teucrium was used in ancient times for formal hedges 4–5 feet (1.2–1.5 m) high; in modern times, it is less common. Teucrium has lovely foliage, a little sparse, but with a pleasing contrast of dark, bright, and silvery green. Each little leaf is green and smooth on the top of the blade and silver gray and tomentose on the underside. The lavender-blue color of the flowers is a perfect compliment to the foliage. Planted in full sun, these plants resist the wind (even sea breezes) and winter temperatures of 30° F (–1° C). They tend to grow in a somewhat messy fashion, with long shoots that have few leaves. Therefore, they require rather drastic pruning, shortening the branches by at least two-thirds at the beginning of spring (March–April) and repeating the cutting once or twice during the summer.

Viburnum

(*Caprifoliaceae*: *Viburnum propinquum*, *V. tinus*, *V.t.* 'Eve Price', *V.t.* 'Lucidum', *Viburnum davidii*, Zones 8–10) The evergreen viburnum is an elegant shrub, ideal for making standards, rounded topiaries, and hedges 6–10 feet (1.8–3 m) high in the case of the *V. tinus* and 3–5 feet (1–1.5 m) high in the case of *V. davidii*. The leaves are mid-sized, leathery, bronze green, dark, and glossy on top, lighter and duller on the underside. The lovely white pinkish flowers grow in bunches and are fragrant some of the time. The laurustinus (*V. tinus*) and its varieties are particularly interesting because they flower abundantly from fall to the end of spring. The small fruit have a brilliant metallic blue tone when ripe. They are present when the buds begin to turn pink and open. Viburnum is hardy, more so than is commonly believed. In the case of laurustinus, it withstands temperatures of 20° F (–6 ° C), although it can be damaged by cold wind. To protect it, plant it in a sheltered location. These plants grow in any kind of soil—even in alkaline or poor, dry soil—at the foot of large trees, by the sea, in the sun and in partial shade. In full shade, however, they tend to grow less thick and to flower less. Prune at the end of the blooming period.

Boxwood

The boxwood and the yew are excellent topiary plants. The boxwood, with its evergreen, glossy foliage, can create hedges, borders, and sculptures of the most complex shapes. Although it changes, it is always understated. Depending on the desired result, you can use different species and varieties of boxwood.

(Buxaceae: Buxus balearica, Zones 8–10; B. microphylla, Zones 6–8, some varieties hardy in Zone 5; B.m. 'Compacta', B. sempervirens, B.s. 'Rotundifolia', B.s. 'Suffruticosa', Zones 6–8) Depending on the variety, the boxwood can be a small tree, a dwarf, or a medium-sized shrub. Very slow growing and very long-lived, it is suited for borders, even those only 8 inches (20 cm) high, using the dwarf varieties or, more commonly, hedges that are $2\frac{1}{2}$–4 feet (0.8–1.2 cm) high; greater heights are reached over very long periods of time. Boxwood is the ideal plant for formal hedges because it maintains active buds even on very old wood. This means the plant stays completely covered in leaves and remains constantly at the desired height. Neglected plants or plants damaged by severe pruning are easily rejuvenated. This hearty plant encourages the most imaginative shapes of topiary art. The leaves are small, glossy, leathery, and more or less dark green or variegated, depending on the variety. Boxwood is suited to any type of soil, even to the very dry soil usually found at the base of large trees, and to any kind of exposure, sun or shade. The hardiest species is B. microphylla, which withstands winter temperatures up to 14° F (−10° C). This is followed by B. sempervirens and B. balearica. From the beginning of spring to the end of summer, trim the plants one to three times, depending on the degree of perfection you want.

Herbs

Aromatic herbs have been associated with topiary art since ancient times. We find them in simple medieval flower beds, in complex English knot gardens, and in elaborate French designs. Today, as in the past, they are the ideal complement to small parterres in aromatic gardens.

Because of their tiny or medium-sized foliage, herbs are suitable for small green sculptures that can be grown in pots. The variety of leaf colors makes them useful in all aspects of the formal garden, from low borders to parterres to designs displaying the full range of greens, grays, or silvers, as well as golds and purples. Adding to the visual pleasure of design and color is the important element of fragrance, which is evident even when only standing near them or brushing past them. Over the centuries, people have felt that herbs were beneficial for their health and their spirit. All herb plants are robust. Because of their thin and deep roots, they thrive even in poor and superficially dry soil, as long as the soil is cool deep down and well drained. To grow compact and orderly, plant them in full sun.

Hyssop
(*Labiatae*: *Hyssopus officinalis*, Zones 3–9) Hyssop is a small shrub suited to making low borders 12–20 inches (30–50 cm) high with a square or rounded contour and to making isolated topiaries in spheres or semi-spheres. The thin and glossy dark green leaves are evergreen or partially evergreen, depending on the harshness of the winter. Hyssop is hardy and tolerates alkaline soils. It also thrives by the sea. Prune in spring, keeping only a few inches (cm) of the wood from the previous year. If necessary, prune a second time at the height of summer. According to tradition, hyssop purifies places and souls.

Lavender
(*Labiatae*: *Lavandula angustifolia* and varieties, Zones 5–8; *L. dentata*, Zones 8–9; L. stoechas, Zones 8–9) Commonly used for low, rounded borders 1–3 feet (30–90 cm) high or for isolated topiaries in a ball or semi-spherical shape, lavender can also be made into a standard. The narrow, elongated, pointed leaves are green, dentate, and rounded at the top in *L. dentata*, the least hardy species. The color of the spikes, the sizes, and the blooming periods vary according to the species and variety. For example, some dwarf lavenders, such as *Lavandula* 'Hidcote', are no higher and wider that 1 foot (30 cm). In addition, some lavenders have blue, violet, sky-blue indigo, purple, pink, or white flowers. To appreciate the fresh perfume and the relaxing power of the flowers, you must violate the rules of topiary art which demand a summer pruning to maintain the perfectly geometric shape. Instead, leave it to flower. At the end of this period, or at least at the end of the summer, prune it, cutting the spikes that have withered an inch or so (3–4 cm) below the top of the plant. You can rejuvenate neglected and overly bare plants with a drastic pruning at the beginning of spring.

Rosemary
(*Labiatae*: *Rosmarinus officinalis*, *R.o.* 'Fastigiatus', Zones 8–10) Rosemary, one of the most typical Mediterranean plants, was frequently used in ancient times in topiary art because of its adaptability and beauty. But it was also used for its symbolic meaning, which was associated with loyalty. It creates low or medium

borders 3–5 feet (1–1.8 m) tall and standards or green sculptures on frames. The foliage is evergreen, very rich, and bright in all the varieties. The leaves are thin and glossy; the flowers, small and light blue in the typical species, but they can also be white or pink. Fairly hardy, rosemary withstands 30° F (−1° C) for short periods, if placed in a sheltered position. It should be pruned regularly, shortening the vegetation of the preceding year by one-half to one-third. Avoid making cuts that are too drastic because rosemary has some difficulty revegetating from very old wood.

Rue

(*Rutaceae*: *Ruta graveolens*, Zones 4–8) This small suffruticose plant is suited for low borders 1–3 feet (30–80 cm) high, standards, and rounded green sculptures. The pretty evergreen leaves, an unusual bluish green, are considered helpful for chasing away witches. Rue is hardy and grows in any type of soil, but it prefers soil that is slightly alkaline and clayish, in full sun. Prune in spring, shortening the vegetation of the previous year by one-half to one-third. Prune again in summer to remove the floral tops.

Sage

(*Compositae*: *Salvia officinalis*, Zones 5–8) Sage is used in parterres, borders 1–2 feet (0.3–0.70 m) tall with rounded contours, and isolated semi-spherical topiaries. Like santolina, sage is suited for design flower beds because of the play of color in the leaves. Its medium evergreen leaves are oval and fleshy in shades of gray green, golden yellow, and purple or variegated with white, green, and pink. A scanty shrub in full sun, it is hardier than rosemary, withstanding temperatures up to 20° F (−6° C). It tends to grow in a messy fashion and become woody, so prune it often. In spring, shorten the vegetation of the previous year by one-half to one-third; in summer, trim the current vegetation once or twice. If it becomes messy, you can reshape it with a drastic pruning, cutting it back to a height of 16–20 inches (40–50 cm).

Santolina—Lavendar Cotton

(*Compositae*: *Santolina chamaecyparissus, S. virens*, Zones 6–8) Like lavender, myrtle, hyssop, and rosemary, santolina has been used in topiary since antiquity to create small borders 1–2 feet (30–60 cm) high, designs, and parterres playing on the color contrast of the different species. The small evergreen leaves are linear and finely dentate. They can be bright green or silver gray, nearly white. Prune them at the beginning of spring and again in summer to avoid the production of the flower, which would destroy the neat appearance of the foliage. Santolina is hardy and grows well in all soils, even poor soil, whether it is slightly acidic or alkaline.

Thyme

(*Labiatae*: *Thymus, T. vulgaris*, Zones 4–8) Thyme is a lovely little plant with tiny, evergreen, fleshy smooth, tomentose leaves which are gray green or variegated with white or golden yellow. Thyme is said to keep away melancholy. It creates very low borders 6–10 inches (15–25 cm) high and miniature topiaries, usually as standards or sphere shapes. Hardy and adaptable to varied climates, it thrives in all types of soil, even very poor soil.

Conifers

Like bonsai and orchids, conifers are either much loved or cordially despised. Whatever your personal taste, only some of them are suited to topiary art. In fact, pine trees and fir trees do not have the ability to revegetate along the branches, while yews, cypresses, junipers, *Chamaecyparis*, tsugas, and thujas are well suited because they can tolerate frequent pruning.

Yew, cypress, and juniper belong to the tradition of topiary. In the Mediterranean region, the cypress was one of the first plants to be used to sculpt plant shapes. Thujas, *Chamaecyparis*, and *Cupressocyparis*, more recently introduced, are often used to create formal hedges because they grow very rapidly. You'll want to consider the different species and varieties, keeping in mind that the darker tones will offset other possible colors in the garden more than the lighter tones will. Conifers are recommended if you want to design closed spaces to plant flowers. Species or varieties of glaucous green or even light blue are very difficult to match, resulting in a rather unconnected appearance; they are not recommended for use as entire hedges.

The species or varieties with golden leaves are useful for particular color contrasts in large gardens.

Chamaecyparis— False Cypress

(*Cupressaceae*: *Chamaecyparis lawsoniana*, Zones 5–8; *C. nootkatensis*, Zones 4–8; *C. obusta*, Zones 4–8; *C. pisifera*, Zones 4–8; and their cultivars) These are large trees suited to making large green sculptures and hedges over 10 feet (3m) high and at least 3–4 feet (1–1.2 m) thick. Varying in size, shape, and leaf color, the countless varieties often develop naturally in a globe or cone shape that is easy to sustain with light yearly trimmings. These plants grow best in soil that is rich in humus and cool, but also alkaline, and in areas that are not very humid in the winter, in which case they become less compact and neat. They withstand wind, including sea breezes.

Prune in late spring and, if necessary, during the summer. Remove the vegetation of the current year and the small branches of the previous year, but do not prune the old wood. Allow it to reach its final height before beginning to model it into the desired shape.

Cypress— Monterey Cypress, Italian Cypress

(*Cupressaceae*: *Cupressus macrocarpa, C. sempervirens*, Zones 7–9) The *Cupressus sempervirens*, a traditional topiary art plant, is used for hedges at least 10–26 feet (3–8 m) tall, espaliers, windbreaks, exedrae, spirals, carved signs, etc. Pliny the Younger said, "You can make walls, and it can be chosen to portray hunts and ships and other things." Hardy, but a little slow to develop, it grows in all soils, even alkaline, as long as it is well drained. It withstands the wind well. The *C. macrocarpa* prefers the light and sandy soil found in coastal areas. It is not very hardy, but it grows quickly. Both of these plants are pruned in late spring and in summer. Limit the cutting to one or two years' vegetation.

At right, topiary shapes made of yew (Taxus baccata) *in poplar bark containers. Extremely elastic, this plant can also be grown in pots, as long as the soil is well drained.*

Leyland Cypress

(*Cupressaceae*: x *Cupressocyparis leylandii*, Zones 5–9) The
Leyland cypress is a large tree that was created
in the nineteenth century by crossing two species
belonging to different genuses: *Cupressus macrocarpa*,
which gave it the shape of the foliage, and *Chamaecyparis
nootkatensis*, which gave it the light green color. These
plants grow quickly and maintain a compact pyramid
shape naturally. They are especially useful for making
espaliers 10 feet (3 m) tall and higher and 3–4 feet (1–1.2
m) thick and for making large green sculptures. Hardy and
free of diseases, they stand up well to pruning. Trim at the
height of vegetation and, if need be, again during the
summer.

Juniper

(*Cupressaceae*: *Juniperus chinensis*, *J.
communis*, Zones
3–8; *J.* x
media, *J.
sabina*, *J.
squamata*, *J.
virginiana*,
and varieties,
Zones 4–8) Trees
or large shrubs of
different bearing, junipers
can easily be grown in many
shapes, in standards, and in
hedges 5–6 feet (1.5–2 m)
tall. Several varieties
naturally take on a global
or conical shape.
Although their extreme
plasticity is not matched
by an equal aesthetic value, junipers enjoy great favor for
their particularly fast growth and economy as compared to
more beautiful topiary plants. Hardy and wind resistant,
they grow in all kinds of well-drained soil, even very
alkaline, and in full sun. Prune in late spring and in
summer.

Yew

(*Taxaceae*: *Taxus baccata*, Zones 5–9; *T.* x *media*, Zones;
4–9; and varieties) The yew lends itself to all of the most
fantastic
inventions
of topiary
art and is unparalleled in the
formal garden for building
green walls and dividing
spaces geometrically. As is the
case with boxwood, the list of
shapes that have been made
could fill entire pages. Over the
centuries, teams of enthusiastic
gardeners have sculpted angels, gods, entire mythological
scenes, episodes of war, objects of daily use, furnishings,
modes of transportation, and animals out of yew trees—
not to mention all the possible simple geometric shapes
and their combinations. In the last four centuries, the yew
has replaced boxwood as the topiary plant of choice in
many countries because it grows faster and larger.
The yew is mistakenly believed to be a very slow plant. In
fact, a yew hedge can grow 12–16 inches (30–40 cm) a
year—approximately twice as much as boxwood, although
this is about half the growth of other popular evergreens.
Even if the initial cost of planting is high, the quality of the
final result is incomparable with any other species. The
yew can be made into thin, compact hedges, as well as
thick and tall hedges 6–13 feet (1.8–4 m) high. The
evergreen foliage is compact and made of short, flattened,
very dark, glossy needles. It matches all the other possible

shades of green in the garden and creates an excellent background for any flowers. There are also several varieties of yellow or golden foliage which create color contrasts with the typical shape. Other varieties naturally take on a narrow column shape and require only light cuttings to maintain a full and even shape.

The yew grows well in soils with excellent drainage that are dry deep down. It also does well in alkaline soil, preferably rich in humus. Prune regularly, beginning from late spring through the entire summer. The frequency of the cutting depends on the degree of perfection demanded; one single cutting may be sufficient, but, in general, at least two are needed. If the plant is old and woody, you may need to resort to a drastic renewal pruning in the spring, cutting as far as the old wood, which may still have active buds and can cover the plant with new vegetation quite quickly. A generous application of nutrient rich in organic matter, such as manure, should accompany such a pruning.

Thuja

(*Cupressaceae*: *Thuja occidentalis*, Zones 4–7; *T. orientalis*, Zones 6–9; *T. plicata*, Zones 5–8; and varieties) Thujas are trees or shrubs, suited for hedges 6–14 feet (1.8–4 m) tall and above and at least 3–4 feet (1–1.2 m) thick. They are also suited for large green sculptures. The evergreen foliage is very compact and occurs in many different shades of green or variegated colors. As with many other conifers, some varieties have a naturally conical or globular shape. These plants grow quickly in all types of cool, deep soil that is not overly dry, even in positions which are exposed to the wind. Prune in late spring and, if necessary, again at the height of summer. As is the case with *Chamaecyparis lawsoniana*, let the top of the plant reach the desired height before beginning to trim it in the predetermned shape.

Tsuga

(*Pinaceae*: *Tsuga canadensis*, Zones 4–7; *T. heterophylla*, Zones 6–9) Large majestic trees, the tsugas make magnificent hedges 8–13 feet (2.5–4 m) tall and higher and at least 4 feet (1.2 m) thick. Frequently used in North America, where they originated, they possess the same elegance, plasticity, and regenerative ability as does the yew tree. They resist wind, even cold wind, but they prefer a climate with humid winters, in cool, deep, rich soil that is even slightly alkaline. Prune in late spring; once shaped, trim the hedges once or twice during the summer.

Golden Conifers

The species and varieties of conifers with variegated or golden leaves are very useful in creating particular color contrasts for large gardens. The most ornamental ones, for example, are *Cupressus macrocarpa* 'Goldcrest' (Zones 8–10), *Cupressocyparis laylandii* 'Castlewellan Gold' (Zones 5–9), *Taxus baccata* 'Aurea' (Zones 5–9), *Juniperus* x *media* 'Pfitzerana Aurea' (Zones 4–8), *Chamaecyparis lawsoniana* 'Lanei', *C.l.* 'Stewartii', and *C.l.* 'Ellwood's Gold' (Zones 5–8).

Geometric shapes created with Cupressus macrocarpa *'Goldcrest'*.

Fruit Trees

The custom of growing fruit trees in set shapes is a very old one, and the reason is not simply aesthetic. In fact, when fruit trees are dwarfed, they start producing earlier and they produce more fruit. In addition, the fruit benefits from optimal exposure to the sun's rays because of the artificial arrangement of the branches.

Over the years, different methods of growing fruit trees were developed and codified. These rules are still used in growing fruit. By using pots, pyramids, spindles, and espaliers (usually trained against a wall), we can grow species that are not very hardy. Some of the varieties that need long, warm summers in order to bear fruit benefit from the espalier method because the heat released from the wall encourages growth. This also encourages fruit production to begin early and helps the fruit reach maturation early. The main characteristic of plants trained on an espalier is their development in only two dimensions: height and width.

Apple Tree

(*Rosaceae*: *Malus communis*, Zones 4–9) The apple tree can reach a height of 32–50 feet (10–15 m), but it will only grow to be 6–16 feet tall (2–5 m) if you graft it on dwarf stock. It bends to different growing shapes, such as the espalier, U, Y, candelabrum, growing freely or against a supporting wall. It is suited to nearly all kinds of soil, except those that are too alkaline or too damp.

Apricot Tree

(*Rosaceae*: *Prunus armeniaca*, Zones 5–9) The apricot tree is an attractive free-form tree that does not exceed 23–26 feet (7–8 m) in height and 13–16 feet (4–5 m) in the diameter of the foliage. It is usually grown free-form because it does not withstand drastic pruning. In mountainous regions, it is occasionally trained on an espalier or fan against the wall of a house. Despite being hardy, it shuns cold winds and late frosts in spring that can damage its early bloom.

Cherry Tree—Sweet Cherry Tree, Sour Cherry Tree

(*Rosaceae*: *Prunus avium*, Zones 4–8; *Prunus cerasus*, Zones 4–8) are usually grown free-form. The sweet cherry tree reaches 32–50 feet (10–15 m) in height and 26–32 feet (8–10 m) in diameter; the sour one reaches 13–16 feet (4–5 m) in height and the same in diameter. You can train them on an espalier or fan against supporting walls.

They withstand low temperatures very well and are not usually damaged by late spring frosts. The sour cherry tree is a tough plant that grows in clayish and sandy soils; the sweet cherry tree is more demanding and requires fertile, cool, and well-drained soil.

European Plum Tree and Japanese Plum Tree

(*Rosaceae*: *Prunus domestica*, Zones 5–8) Plum trees grow as high as 23–32 feet (7–10 m) tall. Because they have a surface root system, they need well-drained soil that is not overly dry. In areas subject to spring frosts, cultivate the American varieties instead of the Japanese because they blossom later. The most frequent training shapes are the natural spindle or pyramid, the pot, the frame, and, in areas with severe winter weather, the espalier against the wall.

Fig Tree

(*Moraceae*: *Ficus carica*, Zones 7–10) The fig tree is a plant that likes a mild climate and long, warm summers. In areas with harsh winter climates, you can train it in the shelter of a southern exposed wall, where it can reach 19–23 feet (6–7 m) in height. Since it does not withstand pruning well, if you are training it against a wall, guide it by lightly pruning the young lateral branches. These trees prefer dry soil that is cool deep down.

Grapevine

(*Vitaceae*: *Vitis vinifera*, Zones 6–10) Although it is hardy, late spring frosts and winter temperatures below 10° F (−12° C) damage the grapevine. These plants are suited to climates with long, warm summers that allow an optimal ripening of the fruit. The grapevine is the

perfect plant for pergolas, but itis equally beautiful on a free espalier or an espalier against a wall. This last kind of training is only suggested in areas with a very severe winter climate. With cool and airy summers, plan an appropriate distance, 4–6 inches (10–15 cm), between the plant and the wall or the poor air circulation between the leaves will encourage the proliferation of fungal diseases.

Olive Tree

(*Oleaceae*: *Olea europaea*, Zones 9–10) Typical of Mediterranean regions and climates, the olive tree is a very long-lived plant that can reach 65 feet (20 m) in height and 19–32 feet (6–10 m) in diameter. It withstands rather low temperatures, provided the onset is not too sudden. It prefers cool and well-drained soil, but it adapts to stony, alkaline, and dry soil. Typically grown free-form, it also lends itself to being trained on a frame or in a pot.

Peach Tree

(*Rosaceae*: *Prunus persica*, Zones 5–9) The peach tree reaches 13–19 feet (4–6m) in height and has a round shape. It is typically trained in a pot or on a frame. To protect it from the winter cold and from spring frosts, you can train it against a wall. In this case, the most suitable shape would be the fan. It has a rather superficial root apparatus and, therefore, tends to suffer from dryness in the summer. It grows in well-drained soil and can be cultivated in alkaline soil only if grafted on an almond tree. Peach trees thrive in a mild climate where the summers are not excessively warm and the winters are not too severe. However, winters must be cold enough to allow an adequate vegetative dormant period for the development of flower buds.

Pear Tree

(*Rosaceae*: *Pyrus communis*, Zones 5–8) The pear tree can reach 50 feet (15 m) in height and 23–26 feet (7–8 m) in diameter. The foliage keeps its pyramidal shape when it reaches maturity. Like the apple tree, it is frequently trained on an espalier, often on dwarf stock. Very high summer temperatures can damage it, and it prefers humid and mild climates.

Citrus Trees

During the Renaissance, the Medicis were the first to collect citrus trees. Since then, in their large terra-cotta pots, they have become a characteristic element of the Italian garden. The famous "orangeries," fashionable in the seventeenth century, were constructed so that the citrus trees could be grown in cold climates.

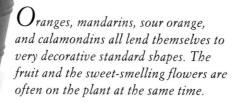

Oranges, mandarins, sour orange, and calamondins all lend themselves to very decorative standard shapes. The fruit and the sweet-smelling flowers are often on the plant at the same time.

Citrus Trees

(*Rutaceae*, Zones 10–11) The orange
(*Citrus sinensis*), the lemon (*Citrus limon*),
the mandarin (*Citrus nobilis*), the
kumquat (*Fortunella* sp.), the bitter
orange (*Citrus myrtifolia*), and the
calamondin (*Citrus mitis*) are small
evergreen trees typical of regions with
temperate, warm, and subtropical
climates. They vegetate well outdoors in
areas where winter temperatures do not go
below about 40° F (5° C); in many North
American regions and in large areas of
Europe, they should be cultivated in pots
and taken into a cold house during the
winter. Since they can be damaged by
wind, place them in sheltered areas. Some
varieties of lemon and bitter orange are
more resistant to cold than other citrus
plants; therefore, you can grow them in
the ground in the shelter of a wall with a
southern exposure, which provides
adequate winter protection.
Citrus trees love loose, cool soil enriched
with organic matter. Usually, we train
them on a standard frame or an espalier.
When they are potted, the espalier should
be round, created by leaning the branches
on a circular support trellis.

*Lemon trees are usually trained on a standard or on a flat
or circular espalier. Rounded espaliers help to shelter them
during the coldest months.*

Flowering Trees

Training flowering climbers and shrubs on a standard frame is a very old custom. Although roses, fuchsia, and pelargonium have been grown in this way for a long time, the move to exotic species is rather recent, and in the majority of our regions, they need protection during the winter in porches, cold houses, or similar environments.

Flowering trees are very decorative, especially during the flowering period. As with any other plant grown in this shape, they are something special in a pot. However, they lose a large part of their charm if planted directly in the ground. In fact, they look ridiculous in the ground.

Climbing plants or shrubs are created by grafting them on stock or by allowing them to grow until the trunk without branches or leaves reaches a certain height. Depending on the fashion or the season, plants with very different characteristics and requirements may be available. Azaleas, *Laburnum*, lilac, broom, *Buddleia*, *Hydrangea*, *Wisteria*, and roses can stay outdoors all year round. On the other hand, *Bougainvillea*, *Callistemon*, *Cestrum*, *Cassia*, *Feijoa*, *Fuchsia*, *Hibiscus*, *Lantana*, *Marguerite*, *Plumbago*, *Polygala*, and *Solanum* must spend the winter in a cold house or in a sheltered place with good exposure. Finally, although *Datura*, *Abutilon*, *Pelargonium*, and *Tibouchina* can stay in the house throughout the year, taking them outside in the summer helps the wood mature; as a result, they flower more abundantly the following season.

Recently, the choice of species and varieties used to create flowering standards has continued to grow.

The Leptospermum scoparium, *from Australia, can be trained in the shape of a standard because of its tiny leaves and the plentiful and long flowering period. Like the laurel, it withstands the cold only when the growth has ripened.*

Polygala myrtifolia, *from South Africa, flowers almost year round; it should be trimmed often to keep it neat and compact.*

A typical plant of the Mediterranean, rosemary was used in topiary in very ancient times to create spheres, standards, and borders.

Climbing Plants

All climbers are considered topiary plants, because they can be trained against a wall with shoots evenly placed on an espalier, a fan, or on many different ornamental motifs. You can create green sculptures with climbers by making them grow on metal frames in geometric, realistic, or imaginary shapes.

This final aspect of topiary art is useful for someone who wishes to achieve rather complicated shapes quickly without having to undertake the task of pruning, a task that demands a certain precision. This method is used in the United States for spectacular creations, often with results of questionable taste, attesting to the extreme pliability of the plants. The custom of training climbing plants on a frame is very old. Originally, it was used to cultivate delicate plants in pots so that they could be taken into the hothouse over the winter. The species chosen, besides those shrubs already mentioned in the general list, are those that lend themselves to this purpose because of their fast growth rate and the shape or compactness of their foliage.

Creeping Ficus

(*Moraceae*: *Ficus pumila*, Zones 7–10) The ficus, with its twisting stalk and compact, tiny, oval, pointed leaves of intense dark green color, is perfect for creating small evergreen sculptures.
In areas with mild winter climates, you can use it to design ornamental motifs, even very elaborate ones, on entire walls. The ficus is delicate, surviving outdoors only in areas where the temperature does not go below 40–45° F (4–8° C). It needs well-drained soil and full shade.

Honeysuckle

(*Caprifoliaceae*: *Lonicera sempervirens*, *L. japonica*, Zones 4–9) There are many species and varieties of honeysuckle with yellow, white, red purple, and orange flowers. All are very fragrant and very hardy. Because these plants are quite vigorous, you can make flowering standards with the trunks supported by a pole and green sculptures on fairly sturdy frames. You can grow them in the sun or in bright shade in well-drained soil.

Ivy

(*Araliaceae*: *Hedera colchica*, *H. colchica dentata*, *H. colchica* 'Variegata', *H. helix*, *H. helix* 'Aureo-variegata', 'Buttercup', 'Discolor', 'Goldheart', 'Jubilee', 'Silver Queen', 'Tricolor'…, Zones 6–9) There are many varieties of ivy with leaves that are more or less entire or lobed and variegated with cream, yellow, silver white, or purple pink. We use them to cover walls and metal frames, but we also grow them as shrubs to create formal espaliers. The small-leaf varieties of *H. helix* are better for metal frames because they are well proportioned. They can be grown in any soil, as long as it is cool. They tolerate shade and full light.

Jasmine

(*Oleaceae*: *Jasminium nudiflorum*, Zones 6–10; *J. azoricum*, Zones 9–10; *J. grandiflorum*, Zones 9–10; *J. officinale*, Zones 9–10; *J. polyanthum*, Zones 9–10) As free espaliers or espaliers against a wall, jasmine can also crawl up a geometric frame. If you place it in a very sheltered position, it will blossom with extremely fragrant flowers from mid-spring to late summer. The round espalier, the cone, and the sphere are among the traditional shapes grown in large terra-cotta pots. The only exception is the hardy *J. nudiflorum*, whose primrose yellow flowers appear at the height of winter but have no fragrance.

Muehlenbeckia—Wire Vine

(*Polygonaceae*: *Muehlenbeckia complexa*, Zones 8–10) The very tiny leaves of this climber have a characteristic two-lobe shape. The stem of the plant is very flexible. You can easily train it on even the most complicated frame. A tender plant, it produces little white flowers, followed by red berries that turn black when ripe, as long as it is in a mild weather zone. It likes a soil rich in organic matter and slightly acidic.

Trachelospermum—Star Jasmine

(*Apocynaceae*: *Trachelospermum asiaticum*, *T. jasminoides*, Zones 7–9) Often confused with jasmine because of the small star-shaped, pure white, fragrant flowers, Trachelospermum has earned the nickname "star jasmine." The two have their fragrance and twining in common. An evergreen with lovely dark green, glossy, leathery leaves like the true jasmine, it is magnificent in containers trained on a round espalier or on a cone. Except for regions with particularly severe winters, it is hardy but needs the sun and soil that is rich in organic matter, acidic, and well drained.

At right, a view of Sissinghurst Castle that shows how you can create festoons and designs with roses, clematis, solanum, and jasmine.

Techniques

The following are some techniques
to help you plant, support,
shape, and prune plants to create
and maintain green sculptures.
These techniques and suggestions
will allow you to create traditional
topiary, successfully reproduce
traditional shapes, and think
of new ones.

Implements, Tools, and Accessories

The tools you'll need depend on the shape you're creating or maintaining, the type of vegetation, and the required pruning. Good-quality tools are worth the additional expense because they are significantly more precise and they last longer. In order to safeguard the health of the plant, you must make clean and neat cuts. Keeping your tools in good condition, cleaning them often, oiling them to protect from rust, and sharpening them from time to time will protect your plants, as well as the tools.

*F*or higher branches, you should use the tree pruner. It is stronger that other pruners and can cut even medium-sized branches. It consists of cutting blades mounted on a rod, maneuvered from the bottom by a string.

*F*or small topiaries and branches no larger than $\frac{1}{2} - \frac{3}{4}$ inch (1–2 cm) in diameter, you need to use pruners with a single blade (anvil pruner) or the double-edged version (bypass pruner). The single blade has a straight or curved blade that cuts against a fixed metal edge. Be careful not to squeeze and damage the branch with the counterblade. Double-edge pruners have two curved, convex blades that cut the wood between them. They are more precise, although they are usually more expensive.

*L*ong-handled pruners or loppers can be used to cut fairly thick branches or to reach small branches at greater heights.

*F*or branches 2 ¼–2 ¾ inches (6–7 cm) and even 3–4 inches (8–10 cm) in diameter, you can use a Grecian saw, a small handsaw with a serrated blade.

*H*edge shears have two long, sharp blades. Although you can use them for quick cuts on leaves, young green shoots in small hedges, and small-leaf topiary shapes, they do not allow for much detail.

*F*or thick hedges, use a power hedge trimmer. An electric trimmer is much lighter, but you need a long cord and a power outlet. A gas-powered trimmer allows you complete freedom, but it is heavier. For large-leaf plants, such as the cherry laurel, the laurel, and the holly, you'll have better results using manual shears to cut the small branches above and beneath the leaves. If you use hedge trimmers, the work is rougher and some leaves may be cut in half.

Finally, for renovating adult hedges, you need a saw for the younger branches and a chain saw for those that are more that 4 inches (10 cm) in diameter. You can rent a chain saw.

Planting Hedges and Topiaries

Sculpting plants and hedges in shapes requires time and patience, so it is important to begin with healthy, well-shaped plants that are suited to the local climate and to take special care in planting them.

A hedge can last many decades without needing any special attention. If you are going to use small plants with bare roots, you must plant them during their vegetative dormant period in fall, during the winter, or at its end, depending on the climate. Planting in the fall advances the spring renewal and growth of the plants, but exposes them to the rigors of winter. Thus, in areas with harsh winters, wait for the first warm spell of spring. In hot summer climates, you'll have more success if you plant in the fall or winter because the plants have time to develop a better root system before the onset of warm weather.

You can transplant potted plants, or those that are balled and in burlap bags, at almost any time, except when the ground is frozen and in the summer months unless you can water them often and abundantly.

To make it easier to plant a hedge, work the entire strip of earth you will use, digging a trench $1\frac{1}{2}$–$2\frac{1}{2}$ feet (50–80 cm) wide and $1\frac{1}{4}$–$1\frac{1}{2}$ feet (40–50 cm) deep and removing the weeds. A week before planting, enrich the soil, spreading a layer of approximately 4 inches (10 cm) of manure or other organic fertilizer. In the winter months, transplant during the warmest hours; in the spring months, during the coolest hours. Work as quickly as possible, especially when dealing with plants with bare roots. If for any reason you cannot plant them immediately, or if you are forced to interrupt the operation, you can

Comparison between the wrong way to plant (on the left) and the correct way (on the right). In the first, the roots are not well spread out in the ground, and the neck is buried too deeply; in the second, the roots are nicely spread out, and the neck is at ground level.

temporarily protect the roots from frost and drying out by laying them flat in a deep hole and covering them with soil, sand, or moist peat. For plants with bare roots, cut off the smallest roots since these will die from air exposure, inviting the fungi that cause root rot. Trim the woody roots to stimulate new lateral roots to sprout. If you only have a few plants, dip the roots in a bucket filled with a solution of equal parts of water, clay, and manure for at least half an hour to help them take root. Place the plants in the trench one at a time, taking care to arrange them properly, spreading the roots, making sure that the neck is at ground level. Firmly pack the soil around each plant with your feet so that air pockets do not form. When you have finished, water the plants generously. For the first two or three years following the transplant, continue to water the plants, even during periods of rain: only part of rainwater

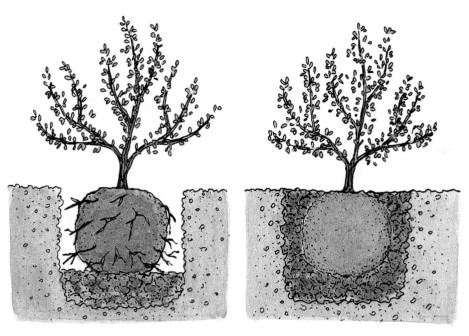

If you place plants in the ground that are balled in burlap bags, the hole must be at least twice as big. The hole must be covered with a layer of organic fertilizer and filled with good soil.

manages to reach the roots, which are not yet well distributed in the earth. In order to reduce the loss of water by evaporation and to eliminate the problem of weeds, mulch the plants, using a dark plastic cloth or a cloth of biodegradable material. In the case of a hedge, spread the cloth on the soil before placing the plants in the ground.

To facilitate the planting of a hedge, work the whole strip of land, digging a trench $1\frac{1}{2}$ –$2\frac{1}{2}$ feet (50–80 cm) wide and $1\frac{1}{4}$ –$1\frac{1}{2}$ feet (40–50 cm) deep and removing the weeds.

Plans for Planting and Distances

To create a predominantly decorative hedge of dwarf boxwood, santolina, hornbeam, beech, or yew, arrange the plants in a single line, evenly spaced. To make a hedge that is protective, dense, and impenetrable, plant them in two lines so that the plants alternate, forming many successive triangles. To ensure that the hedge is well branched from base to top, you can use plants of different heights, arranging the lowest plants in the front row. The distance between the plants is very important for creating a continuous and dense screen. As a general rule, place small shrubs $1\frac{1}{2}$–$2\frac{1}{2}$ feet (40–80 cm) apart, depending upon the vigor of the species, the degree of density, and the effect and degree of compactness desired. Trees, such as hornbeam, maple, and beech, should be planted $2\frac{1}{2}$–5 feet (80–150 cm) apart for a continuous hedge. Even if the hedge seems sparse when you begin, the plants will grow quickly, and in the course of three years, their branches will form a dense screen.

Mulching Against Weeds

To eliminate the problem of weeds that almost inevitably grow in a young hedge, you can use mulch even before planting. Once you have worked the strip of land that will be used for the hedge, dig a border around it. Insert two stakes at either side, at the beginning and at the end. In the case of a particularly long hedge, use a third stake in the middle. Secure the ends of a plastic cloth and spread it out. Bury the borders. With a hoe, make openings in the cloth, as many as there are plants. At the set distance, dig corresponding holes. Insert a plant in each and press the soil around the neck.

*T*o protect the neck and avoid the appearance of weeds in the portions of earth left uncovered by the torn cloth, pile leaves, peat, sawdust, or other mulching material at the base of each plant.

*A*t the Villa Serbelloni in Bellagio, Italy, towering cones of yew act as a counterpoint to the horizontal lines of the terraces and to the curved lines of the spherical sculptures in a superb play of green tones.

Pruning

Pruning a plant fosters denser growth and gives it a planned shape. The two types of pruning are shaping and maintenance pruning.

Pruning a hedge or any other topiary plant at regular intervals allows you to maintain the desired shape and to stimulate lateral shoots to sprout. This encourages the plant to grow dense and well branched even in the lower part, rather than to widen in all directions. Each time the branches or twigs of a plant are shortened, the development is controlled, and the plant is forced to issue many new lateral shoots, forming a dense and thick foliage. Cutting a branch a little above the bud stimulates the development of a shoot in the direction indicated by the point of the bud. Thus, you can force plants to assume desired shapes and to make them become two-dimensional. However, pruning the leaves slows down the development of the roots, and if the cuts are too severe and in too close, they can weaken the plant. With young plants, prune lightly at regular intervals, make small cuts, and remove new vegetation. The young plant can then react more readily to the loss of reserve material. It is dangerous to prune near or during the period of frosts. New shoots, which could form as a reaction to the pruning, may die, and the parts of branches beneath the cut may dry up, opening the way for pests and diseases.

The different shades of green create an ideal background for the flowers in this detail of the Villa Gamberaia in Settignano.

Plants That Withstand Rejuvenation

Hedges with irregular growth, stripped at the base or misshapen, can be renewed with a rather drastic pruning treatment at the end of winter, just before plant renewal. The cut may be up to a few inches (cm) from the main woody stems in some types of plants (hornbeam, beech, privet, holly, laurel, boxwood, ilex, berberis, camellia, lavender, pyracantha, viburnum, yew) that are undamaged by this kind of treatment. In all other cases, you should only prune with a cleaning cut to remove the dead parts and only cut the vegetation of the last two or three years. Abundant and frequent fertilization will foster the development of new vigorous vegetation. The following year, trim the shoots that develop once again 3–4 inches (8–10 cm) from the previous cutting. Pests can easily attack the new vegetation.

Pruning to Shape Hedges

For topiary hedges to be beautiful, they must be compact and dense from top to bottom. Pruning to shape helps to achieve this because clipping the tops of plants can prompt greater development of the underlying small branches.

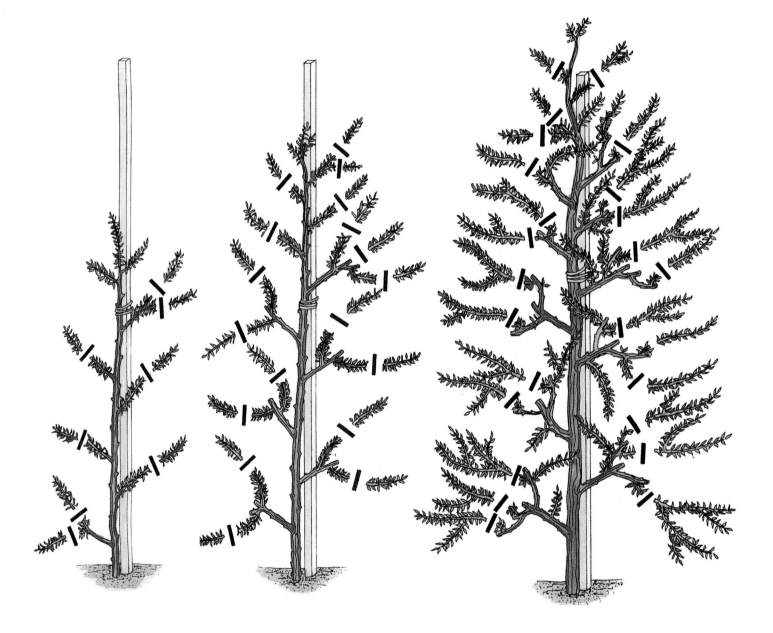

Pruning Conifers

Conifers need to be treated differently because they can grow in height only if the terminal shoot is preserved. They are, therefore, left to grow until they reach their final height; the lateral branches that are too long are clipped. Once

shaped, conifer hedges usually stay neat, with a trimming once during the summer, but for the more vigorous species such as yew and hemlock, two trimmings are needed, generally in June and August. For hedges to produce small branches and leaves, the cut should not be deeper than the vegetation of the last two years.

Trimming Broadleaf Hedges That Tend to Become Sparse at the Base

To shape a beautiful hedge that is dense and that branches well from top to bottom, pay special attention to the pruning for the first two or three years after planting. Among the deciduous plants, several, such as hawthorn, boxwood, privet, and honeysuckle, tend to grow upward, thinning out at the base. They require severe pruning in order to stimulate the production of many low shoots and to create a strong and compact branch structure. At the time of planting, cut the plants 6–8 inches (15–20 cm) from the ground; the following year, cut them 6–8 inches (15–20 cm) from the previous cutting. In subsequent years, as long as the plants are in a phase of vegetative growth, limit the pruning to trimming the new growth. Depending on the species, it will be necessary to intervene two to four times (every four to six weeks) from April to September.

Trimming Broadleaf Hedges That Tend to Interweave

For the large, spreading plants, such as beech, hornbeam, and hazelnut, and for evergreen broadleaf plants that tend to branch out naturally towards the bottom, one lighter pruning during the first two years after planting is sufficient to create a neat structure and to remove untidy branches. Shorten the terminal shoot and longer lateral shoots to one-third of their initial growth. From the third year onward, clip the branches at the top once or twice during the summer to maintain the desired shape and height.

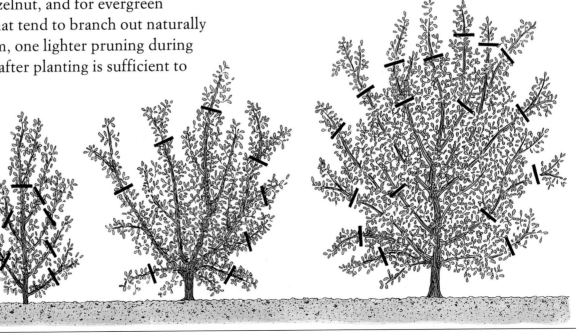

Pruning Adult Hedges

Pruning an adult hedge is artistic work, requiring time and the necessary attention. The first thing to establish is what shape you want: straight, winding, with battlements, or with rounded or pointed edges.

To keep a hedge beautiful, dense, and neat, prune it and fertilize it regularly and, if it snows, remove the snow that collects on it before the weight damages or breaks the branches. Once a hedge is mature, you only need to prune it once or twice a year, around the middle or the end of the summer, so as not to stimulate a strong sprouting of new shoots. You may have to prune at the end of winter to remove the broken and dead branches.

If you need to repair some damage (perhaps a hole has developed) or if you wish to reshape the hedge, you must try to induce strong vegetative growth. To this end, prune deciduous hedges at the beginning of spring and prune conifers and broadleaf evergreens, which are

The Renewal

When hedges are neglected for several years, they lose their formal appearance and become untidy, wide, and empty at the bottom. The branches that are already old and overly woody only produce leaves and young sprouts at their tips. In the majority of these cases, the best thing to do is to uproot them and replace them with young hedges.

A few types, however, such as holly, laurel, cotoneaster, pyracantha, myrtle, and yew, are salvageable since they can tolerate the severe pruning necessary for the vegetation to renew itself. This renewal pruning is done in the spring to stimulate a strong production of shoots at the end of winter, shortly before growth resumes for deciduous plants and at the end of spring for evergreens.

Cut all the branches on one side just before the trunk, and, the following year (or after two years), repeat the procedure on the other side. After the pruning, you can help the hedge's renewal with generous waterings and fertilizers rich in nitrogen.

slower to produce new growth, in mid- to late spring. The frequency of pruning varies, depending on the speed of growth and the desired level of perfection, from two to three times to five to six in the case of vigorous plants, such as privet, honeysuckle, and teucrium. If the hedge was made with parallel sides, begin by pruning indiscriminately from the vertical sides or from the top. If it is tapered, start from the top; if the hedge is very wide, trim it first from one side and then from the other.

To prune a hedge correctly, use special tools, such as a carpenter's level and an adjustable builder's square.

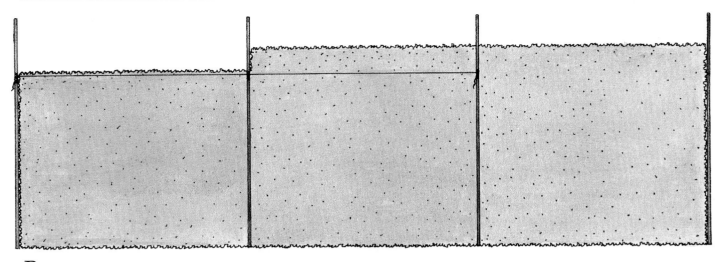

PRUNING AN ADULT HEDGE WITH
PARALLEL SIDES
*Once you've decided on the height of
the hedge, place a few sticks by the
sides, inserting them into the ground*
*two by two. Starting from one end,
space them evenly at least 6½ feet (2 m)
apart. Check that the sticks are
perpendicular to the ground, using a
spirit level you rest on a lath between*
*each pair of sticks. On each stick, mark
a notch corresponding to the desired
height and run a rope from one notch
to another. Then proceed with the
pruning.*

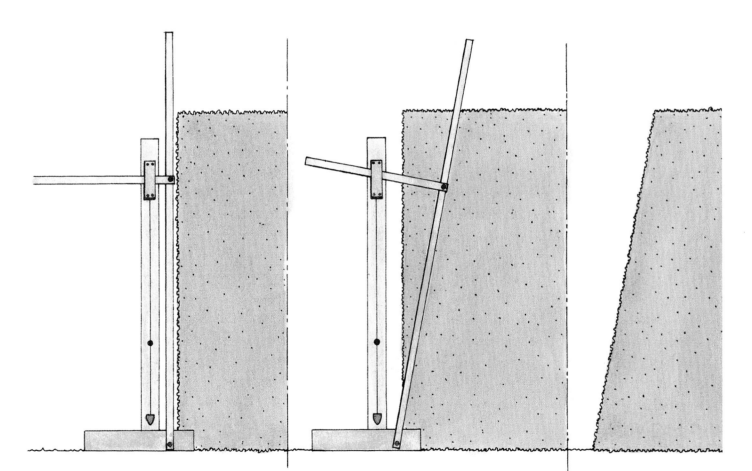

USING AN ADJUSTABLE BUILDER'S
SQUARE
*For cutting hedges into tapered walls,
use an adjustable builder's square. This
is made of a fixed support with wire to
control the vertical angle, which must*
*be verified carefully each time the
instrument is positioned along the
hedge, and a movable shaft hinged at
the bottom. The movable shaft can be
set at the desired angle for the side wall
of the hedge. The angle can be changed,*
*but the most frequently used angle is
approximately 10 degrees and
corresponds to a vertical displacement
of approximately 6–8 inches (15–20
cm) for each 3 feet (1 m) of height of
the hedge.*

How to Fix Mistakes and Flaws

A neglected hedge weakens and withers, but sometimes a hedge that is well cared for may look ruined if it is sick or dried out or simply because it is genetically more sensitive than the other plants.

If the damage is not extensive or if it is fairly recent, you can remedy it by drastically pruning the hedge or its withered part at the end of winter in the case of deciduous plants, or in spring for evergreen plants. This will stimulate the sprouting of new vigorous shoots to correct the damaged parts. Fill in the empty patches caused by the death of a few plants with new plants after removing as much as possible of the soil in which the dead plants were growing, disinfecting the hole, and bringing in new soil.

Outlines and Borders

Hedges can be modeled in many different shapes: the cross section can be rectangular, trapezoidal, pointed, or rounded. Remember that although curved or rounded lines are more difficult to create and maintain than straight and flat ones, they do a better job of hiding mistakes. In any event, formal hedges should always be at least a little tapered on the sides, especially when they are taller than 6 feet (1.8 m), so that the base is wider than the top. In this way, sunlight can easily reach all the foliage, and if it snows, the snow can easily slide off the branches. Ideally the angle should be great enough to be 8 inches (20 cm) off vertical for each 3 feet (0.9 cm) of height. A long, thick hedge lends itself to many ornamental solutions: you can break it up and animate it by digging out variously shaped niches. You can place a statue, a little fountain, or a special plant that you wish to spotlight in each niche.

You can also insert a few short, lower hedges at right angles, designed in such a way that their height decreases towards the center of the garden, with a winding and sloped progression. This will seem to divide the space, even if only subtly, into a series of "rooms," producing intimacy and variety. In the spaces between the main hedge and the successive smaller hedges, you can play with the arrangement of the plants to your fancy, creating mini gardens sheltered from the wind.

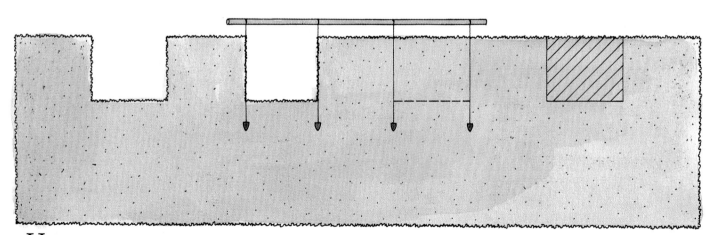

Hᴏᴡ ᴛᴏ Mᴀᴋᴇ Bᴀᴛᴛʟᴇᴍᴇɴᴛs
You can give a hedge a somewhat historical appearance by cutting out battlements or other decorative shapes. Square or rectangular battlements are very easy to create. Use a wooden rod with wires inserted at regular intervals to determine the size of each battlement. When you rest the rod on the hedge, the wires will indicate where and how much to cut.

How to Create Doors, Arches, and Windows

With the same method, and even more simply, you can make doors, windows, and archways in hedges that have already been shaped. Create a template, drive it into the ground at the proper position, lean it up against the hedge, and proceed to cut.

If you decide instead to create an opening, a round window, an arch, or a small doorway in a hedge that is still very young, you should use a metal or wire structure formed in the desired shape. Secure it to the ground or to a strong branch. While the hedge grows around it, you gradually cut the shoots that grow within it.

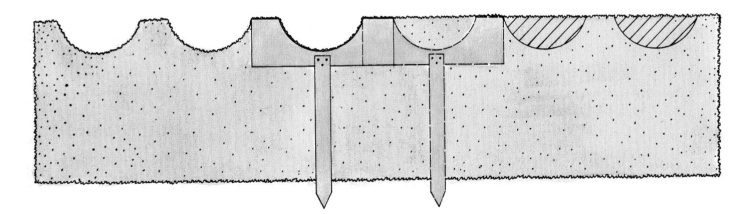

How to Create Waves

To make more elaborate notches—for example, in winding curves—you must construct at least two plywood templates and insert them on supporting sticks with pointed ends. To ensure the evenness of the design, you should insert them in the ground one after the other, leaning them against the hedge so that they are perfectly aligned, with the longer side parallel to the ground. Remove the portion of the vegetation indicated by the first template and then move it past the second one, aligning them once again. Cut the part indicated by the second template and move it past the first one, and so on, until you reach the end of the hedge.

How to Make an Espalier

In addition to all the climbing plants, fruit trees, cotoneaster, pyracantha, *Ceanothus*, magnolia, and laburnum, many other shrubs with pliable branches are sufficiently vigorous and plastic to be trained in different flattened, even shapes.

Since the soil at the foot of a wall is usually drier and less fertile than the rest of the garden, it needs to be worked with care, enriched with humus and various organic fertilizers, watered more often, and, after the planting, mulched to preserve moisture. To shape and support the plants, you can use trellises, wooden or bamboo supports, or, more commonly, wire or plastic frames stretched vertically and horizontally to satisfy the requirements of the particular type of espalier. If you are using plants that are prone to disease, such as fruit plants or roses, you should place the supporting trellis at least 4 inches (10 cm) from the wall to ensure adequate air circulation. In nurseries, you can find species that are already set up on an espalier, and it is easy to maintain the shape with light maintenance pruning. Creating these very flexible and decorative shapes on your own is not particularly difficult, and you will gain a great sense of satisfaction.

In this case, you need to begin with a young plant that has a long main shoot. Plant it 8–12 inches (20–30 cm) away from the wall. Regardless of the shape of the espalier, tie the main shoot to it and then cut it at the height at which you want the branch structure to begin. The following season, many shoots will form. Keep only those necessary for the main branches of the shape, fastening them in turn to the support and cutting the extraneous ones at the base. Continue in this fashion for the next few years, until you achieve the desired branch structure.

The presence of a protecting wall that gives off heat allows you to grow species and varieties which are not very hardy.

To create a fan shape, make a supporting frame, placing wires or wooden rods vertically and horizontally to form a grid and fastening the branches at the points where the wires or rods intersect. Alternately, arrange the wires or rods in a fan shape, giving each the slant that you want the branches to eventually have. Keep all the stronger shoots that are produced during the first season and spread them evenly on the structure. If there are no vigorous shoots, use the best ones available and cut the rest to stimulate the production of other, stronger shoots.

To create a palmette espalier, begin with a small tree that is two or three years old. Tighten the wires that will be used to support future branches. The first wire should be $1\frac{1}{2}$–2 feet (50–60 cm) from the ground and the next ones—two, three, or more—should be spaced 1–$1\frac{1}{4}$ feet (30–40 cm) apart. The first year, before plant renewal, shorten the main shoot to 6–8 inches (15–20 cm) from the ground to prompt it to branch out and cut the lateral branches at the base.

The following year, select three new shoots to form the top shoot and the two side shoots. Attach the first vertically to the supporting wire, slant the other two at a 45-degree angle to the wire, and fasten each one to a rod. Clip the tops of the three buds at the height of the first wire and cut the lateral branches at the base. When the main shoot grows above the second wire, shorten it by approximately 4 inches (10 cm) and remove about 8 inches (20 cm) from the side branches.

The year after that, repeat the procedure. Select three shoots, one as a continuation of the main shoot and two as lateral shoots. Fasten them to the second wire. If you wish to create a third or fourth level, repeat the procedure in the following years. Alternately, clip the main shoot at the height of the third wire and the next year choose two lateral shoots, removing all the others and bending them horizontally, fastening them to the wires. Then shorten them to 8–12 inches (20–30 cm) to stimulate the formation of lateral buds.

Once the espalier is fully formed, remove the supporting rods, cut all the small branches that are extraneous to the shape, clip the tips off the good branches, and proceed with the pruning specified for each species.

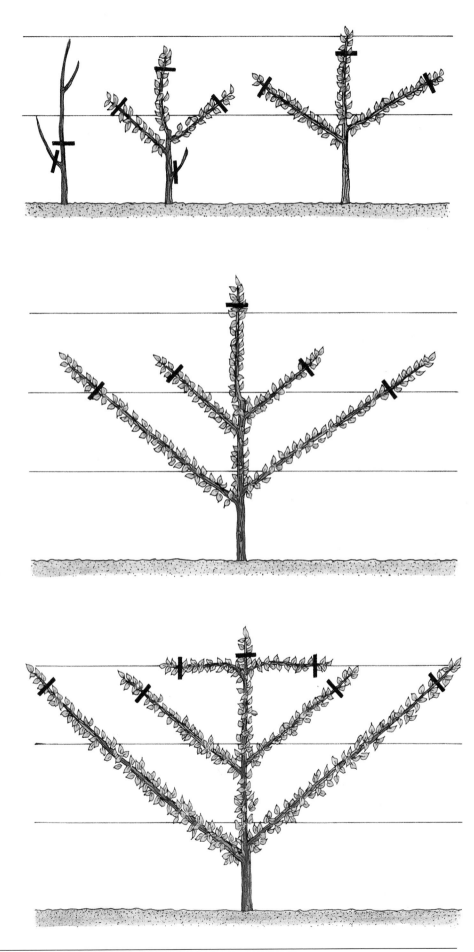

Green Sculptures

For parallel-sided cubes and pyramids, unless you are very skilled or have a template at your disposal, you should use a wire, a spirit level, or if you need to taper surfaces, an adjustable builder's square.

To create an even shape, begin by pruning from the center. Then proceed in two opposite directions simultaneously, always moving from top to bottom and from the center outward. If you work from one part first and then from the other, you'll have a very difficult time making the second side look exactly like the first. For curved surfaces, electric trimmers can be used, but for elaborate shapes with corners and facets, manual shears are much more suitable. In any event, you should always cut with the tip of the scissors because if you use the entire blade, you run the risk of ruining the shape.

A contrast of curved and flat surfaces sculpted in boxwood.

The time needed to make shaped sculptures depends on the desired size and the growth rate of the selected species or variety. You can reduce the amount of time by beginning with plants that are not too young, as long as the shape you are creating allows for slightly older plants. In fact, when using mature plants that have not yet been worked on, start with simple shapes. These are easier and quicker to achieve in this way than by beginning with young plants. You only need to remove the outer foliage and the young wood that is extraneous to the planned shape. To make complex shapes, you need to begin with young plants because once they are mature, they become more difficult to trim, and you run the risk of removing too much foliage. In addition, not all species have the ability to regrow beyond a certain age.

For the first few years, proceed as indicated for pruning a hedge, trying to accentuate the desired shapes. During the formative years, take care of the plants normally: fertilize them at the end of winter. At the onset of winter, protect the less hardy species and varieties, especially those that are potted.

At right, the variety of shapes in the English garden at Levens Hall.

The Sphere

The sphere is the simplest shape to make because the curved lines hide any initial imperfections. The shape can be perfectly spherical, slightly flattened, a little pointed, or egg-shaped.

Start with plants that are four to six years old and already bushy, rounded, and full. To make a boxwood sphere that is 2–2$\frac{1}{2}$ feet (60–80 cm) tall, you need approximately two to three years.

Boxwood is particularly suited to the sphere, especially several of its naturally spherical varieties. *Euonymus*, phillyrea, yew, myrtle, rosemary, laurel, and ilex are also well suited. If the plants are transplanted in the ground, wait one year before starting to prune. The first year after planting, you can trim all the branches in the spring, trying to accentuate the round shape.

In the following years, repeat the procedure until you have reached the desired size. Two or three prunings during the summer are usually enough to maintain the shape. Begin to prune at the highest central part, moving downward along the sides at the same time. Use the points of manual or hedging shears to cut. You can help yourself along with a two-dimensional wooden template resting on two supports with a semicircle cut out of it. Place this on top of the plant and gradually turn it as you cut. The same device can also be used for the cone.

The Cone and the Pyramid

To make a cone or a pyramid, you'll need the same materials as for a sphere. The cone is much easier to create; the pyramid requires perfect symmetry and the same angle for all four sides. Success can only be achieved with the aid of a builder's square.

The procedure for making a cone or a pyramid is similar: both need a supporting structure during the first few years so that they do not become misshapen.

Even the base materials are the same: small plants that are three to four years old or more, depending on the desired height. They should be full and bushy at the bottom and have some central shoots that are already longer than the others, forming a sort of point.

To make the cone, cut the leafy branches in curved lines; for the pyramid, make four tapered triangular surfaces. Among the plants most suited for these shapes are the boxwood, laurel, holly, yew, *Chamaecyparis*, *Thuja*, and juniper.

The Spiral

The spiral is one of the loveliest shapes for isolated topiaries, potted or in the ground. It is a simple shape and, depending on the angle, there is an optical illusion created by the coils: the spiral seems to be continuously in motion, as if it were twisting.

Use evergreen plants that grow upward and have tiny leaves, such as yew, holly, boxwood, *Thuja*, juniper, and *Chamaecyparius*. Start with plants at least $1\frac{1}{2}$–2 feet (50–60 cm) tall that have already assumed an upward shape with a main shoot that is straight and strong. Insert a pole in the center and fasten it, not too tightly, to the main shoot. For the next two years, continue to tie the main shoot to the pole gradually as it grows and, after the winter has passed, shorten all the lateral branches to approximately 4 inches (10 cm) in length. If necessary, repeat the procedure at the end of the summer. When the plant has finally reached 4–$4\frac{1}{2}$ feet (1.2–1.3 m) in height, begin to cut the lower part, shaping it into a spiral. The lowest coil should be longer and wider than the others, while the next ones will be gradually more and more tapered as they move upward. Depending on the growth rate of the plant, you can create an average of one coil per year. When the plant is shaped and holding well, remove the pole.

The Standard and the Ball-Shaped Standard

Ready-made standards, whether simple or composite, are usually grafted on fast-growing stocks that are resistant to disease or specially suited to specific soils.

Without delving into the mysteries of grafting, however, you can train a plant into a standard on your own. Begin with a large one-year-old plant, potted or in the ground. In the spring, cut the young lateral shoots at the base and clip the main shoot at the desired height to get the foliage to start growing. The following year, trim all the new sprouts except three to four buds from the previous cutting. Repeat the same procedure over the following years, creating a sphere that is maintained with light trimmings during the summer. To save time, you can use very young standards and continue to shape them, following the rounded shape of the leaves. The frequency of pruning depends on the species. As long as the plants are young, they'll need pruning in the spring. Once they are shaped, they'll need pruning during the summer.

When planting a standard in the garden, you can create a circular border or a kind of "pot" around it. For example, you can use small plants, such as boxwood or privet, at a distance of 4–6 feet (1.2–1.5 m). Little by little as the standard grows, prune them into a specific shape until they are 2½–3 feet (0.8–0.9 m) high and 1–1½ feet (0.3–0.4 m) thick. Use maintenance prunings in the summer; their frequency depends on the species you've used. For instance, you'll prune less frequently for boxwood and more for privet.

Shapes Made with the Help of Frames

You can make green designs on walls and simple or elaborate figurative shapes, such as rings, hearts, crowns, birds, animals, jugs, or airplanes. Plant them in pots, in the ground, or place them in hedges or on top of other topiary sculptures. There are two techniques; both are reinforced by metal frames.

With the first, described previously, you let the plant grow within the structure, cutting the branches that grow out of it, until the final shape is created and the structure is hidden within it. With the second, similar to the procedure used for climbing plants, you bend and tie the young and pliable shoots to the frame, forcing them to take on its shape; the frame remains empty inside. Depending on the desired shape and the growth rate of the plant used, it takes at least six or seven years to fill out or cover a frame. With the first technique, you can begin with rather mature plants; with the second, the plants must be very young.

The Circle and the Heart

The circle and the heart are simple shapes that are very attractive and easy to create. You begin with a young plant which has two well-developed lateral shoots. In the case of a hedge, you insert a light frame, attaching it to the ground or to the older wood and fastening the two lateral shoots to it.

Over the next years, you continue to tie the shoots to the frame as they grow, removing the small extraneous lateral branches.

The most suitable plants for these shapes are evergreens or semi-evergreens with small leaves, such as boxwood, cotoneaster, privet (*L. delavayanum*), and honeysuckle. Plants like cotoneaster, which are able to flower despite continuous pruning, are especially interesting. Depending on the plants you use, you'll need three to four years to achieve the complete shape.

The Basket

The basket is another rather easy shape
to make, and it is very decorative.
It is best to grow it in a pot
because it does especially well near the house
and serves as a complement when brought
into the garden.

The basket can be used as a furnishing element for the garden, patio, or balcony. You can lay a bunch of cut flowers in it, and, during a party, you can fill it with cherries or strawberries. Begin to shape the basket on a grafted stem, after clipping it at the top and waiting several years for the necessary shoots to develop. With privet, you can finish a basket over the course of two or three years.

The Bird

The bird shape is a little more difficult to make, requiring a greater level of dexterity. You can make a canary, a long-tailed pheasant, a peacock, a long-necked heron, a little duck, etc.

You can create these shapes using three different methods. With the first method, you fill in the structure, trimming the branches that grow out of it; with the second, you tie the new shoots to the structure to make the neck, head, body, and tail. Start with grafted plants, or you can grow them to make a taller or shorter trunk. Trimming the ends of the plants fosters the growth of a good number of shoots. You need to wait at least two years before starting to work on the shape with either of these two methods. The first technique has been previously illustrated; only the shape of the structure changes. To follow the second method, you need a plant that has long, vigorous shoots. Bring a part of the branches together and tie them to make the body. Use a smaller part for the neck and head. A third part forms the tail, which can be long and very narrow or full and wide, depending on the animal you wish to depict. The neck can also be made longer or shorter in this way. Once the plant has taken shape, you need at least another year to fill in the structure. The best results, even though they may take more time, are achieved with evergreen species, such as yew and boxwood, which are more suited for shapes that are planted directly in the ground. The third method is easier and faster. You plant a few bushy plants close together and shape them with the appropriate pruning and tying. For example, to make a bird, you need two plants, one taller and narrower to make the front part of the body and the head, and another shorter to make the back part and the tail, if it is a short tail. You can also use the shorter, more rounded plant for the body and the head and use the tall, narrow plant for the tail. To make a dog or a sheep, you need four plants for the four legs. Gradually, as they grow, you shape the plants into the chosen shape, allowing the two front plants to grow taller to form the head.

Topiaries on Structures

This type of topiary is the fastest and easiest of all because it uses very fast-growing species, such as climbing plants, resting on metal structures. These structures can be of various shapes, from simple to complex: spheres, cones, spirals, obelisks, as well as birds, swans, geese, frogs, and various other animals and figures. You can let your imagination run wild.

In Holland and the United States this technique has been used to create incredible shapes, even entire zoos with elephants, camels, and horses rampant, as well as locomotives, ships, and windmills.

Although there is seldom the risk of overdoing it when creating geometric shapes, it is advisable to use these animated and imaginative shapes with discretion. In fact, they should create an amusing, small surprise; they should not be the principal decorative element in the garden. The simplest method is to plant a climbing plant in the ground or in a pot and let its shoots grow until they are sufficiently long. Then intertwine them and fasten them to the structure, which you have anchored to the ground at several points. A variation of this method, highly suited to species that sprout epigeal roots, such as ivy and *Ficus pumila*, consists of filling in the structure with peat moss to preserve moisture and having the plants grow within it. For large animal shapes, such as horses, lions, and goats, the plants should not start at ground level, especially if you wish to portray them in the act of running or jumping. Insert them in the bottom half of the moss-filled structure; this heightens the illusion that they are "real." Luxuriant species, will take more time and attention to keep them orderly, but less plant know-how.

Topiaries on structures are especially suited to pots placed near or even in the house, perhaps in a porch or in an outdoor sitting area, on the terrace.

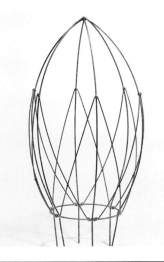

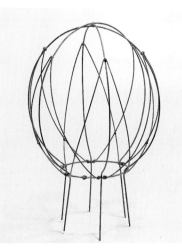

Shapes Made with Structures

To facilitate the creation of a topiary, you can grow it within a structure or frame that you use as a guide in the pruning procedure: you cut everything that grows outside the structure, which will eventually be hidden by the foliage.

This technique is especially suited to architectural shapes (particularly those with geometric and symmetrical sides, such as the pyramid and the obelisk), as well as to bizarre animal shapes and imaginary figures, in the ground or potted, all created with quickly developing species like privet.

For example, to make an obelisk, you construct a frame around the plant, inserting four bamboo sticks in the ground at an angle. Extend metal fencing with average mesh between the sticks. The classic size of an obelisk is $6\frac{1}{2}$ feet (2 m) in height with a square base measuring 2 feet (60 cm) on the bottom and $1\frac{1}{2}$ feet (45 cm) on the top. The sides should be at an 85-degree angle to the ground.

The following year, prune the plant gradually as it develops and its branches poke out of the mesh, leaving just enough so that the fencing gradually disappears.

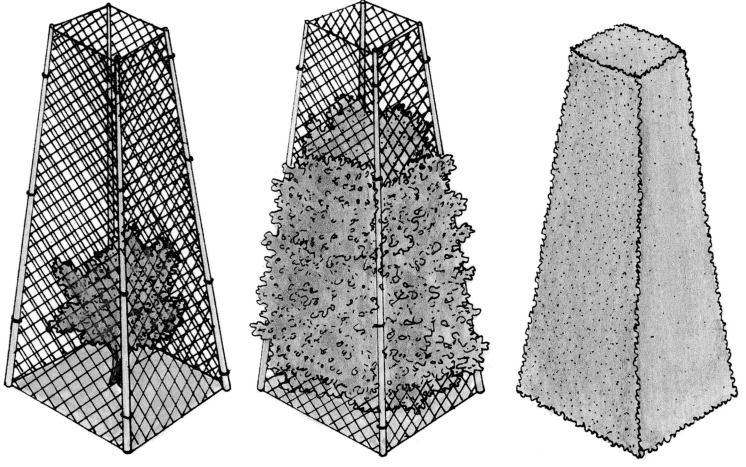

Multi-Tier Shapes

Multi-tier shapes, which look like large green cakes, are rather common decorative elements not only in large historic gardens but also in small private ones. They are quick and easy to make since they are carved out of plants that have already reached a certain size.

You can use an attractive plant from your garden, or plant one especially for this purpose and let it grow until it becomes a small tree or a large shrub. Shape the bottom of the plant, pruning it into a circular shape with a radius that is proportionate to the height of the plant. Strip part of the trunk by removing all the lateral branches. To make the flat part, tie a piece of string that is a little longer than the plant's radius to the trunk and drive a peg into the ground. To cut the edges, tie the outer extremity of the string to the handles of the shears and proceed with the pruning.

To make the next tier, gently fasten a few lateral branches to the base of the trunk with braces so that the branches lie horizontally. Allow the plant to grow until the second tier reaches the desired thickness and the width of the first tier, which has been trimmed to restrict its growth. Shape the other tiers in the following years, until you have created three, four, or five of them. At that point, they should gradually decrease in size. At the top, you can grow a small sphere or some other shape using a metal frame.

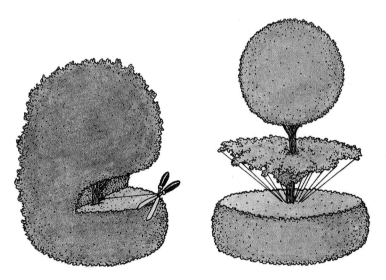

How to Add a Sphere onto a Hedge or Other Topiary Shape

To form a ball on top of a topiary or a hedge, let five or six shoots grow until they reach the height of the desired shape. Continue as previously indicated for shaping the foliage of a standard, trimming the shoots to prompt them to sprout and assume a spherical shape.

You'll need two or three years to build the new sphere on a hedge or other shape and at least that amount of time to fill it in.

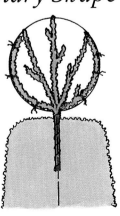

Glossary

Berceae: A pergola.

Branch structure: The structure made up of the body of main and secondary branches of a woody plant.

Grafting: A procedure that joins together parts of two different plants, belonging to different but compatible species or varieties, to make a single unit combining the positive characteristics of both parts.

Humus: A substance or matter, amorphous and brown in color, formed from decomposing organic waste in the earth aided by bacterial forces. It is essential for the soil's fertility, improving its structure, making it more porous, increasing the solubility of minerals, impeding erosion, and stimulating the activity of important microorganisms.

Hybrid: The result of crossing two different species or varieties, naturally or artificially. A hybrid can only multiply by vegetative means (cutting, layering, offshoots).

Main branches: The most important branches, for their age and size, in the branch structure of a woody plant.

Neck: The transitional area between the trunk and the root system. For the health of the plant, especially if it is a woody plant, the neck should be at ground level and never below.

Pole: A small wooden or bamboo stick used to support herbaceous or high shrubby plants, plants with thin trunks, young trees, or newly transplanted shrubs.

Root rot: A change that affects the roots, brought on by parasitic fungi and fostered by poorly structured, compact, and insufficiently airy soil or by mistakes in cultivation.

Shoot: The bud and the part of the branch formed during the current year.

Species: A systematic grouping of all living things that have the ability to be fertile with one another and that have similar physical characteristics.

Stem: A young woody plant, already well rooted, over 6 feet (1.5 m) in height.

Stock: The part of the plant that provides the root system in the grafting process, also called the subject. The part that is grafted, called the scion, object, or graft, provides the aerial portion (branches, leaves, and flowers).

Suffruticose plant: A perennial woody plant, similar to a small shrub, with annual shoots that become woody at the base while the apical parts dry out in winter.

Treillage: A wooden or metal structure on which you can grow climbing plants, fruit trees, or shrubs with very pliable branches trained on an espalier.

Trimming: A light pruning that consists of removing sprouts, flower buds, or the tips of young shoots to stimulate the production of new vegetation, thereby improving the branching and/or flowering.

Trompe l'oeil: Literally an "eye deception," a painting genre that uses false perspectives and views of nature to create the illusion of reality or the perception of widening surroundings.

Variety: A systematic category below that of species or subspecies in which plants are differentiated by one or more traits. A variety can originate naturally or be created through genetic improvement, by crossing different varieties, by natural or induced selection, or by genetic mutation.

Vegetative apex: A group of meristematic or young cells, undifferentiated and able to multiply by division, located at the top of a bud, where all plant tissue begins.

Gardens

This list of gardens for each country cited is not complete. Only a few major gardens and those mentioned in the book are listed.

ITALY
Tuscany
Villa Gamberaia, Settignano (Florence)
Villa Garzoni, Collodi (Lucca)
Villa Marlia, Lucca
Villa La Pietra, Florence
Villa Celsa, Sovicille (Siena)
Villa Gori, Siena
Vicobello, Siena

Lazio
Villa Aldobrandini, Frascati (Rome)
Villa Lante della Rovere, Bagnaria (Viterbo)
Giardini Vaticani, Città del Vaticano (Rome)
Villa La Landriana, Tor San Lorenzo (Rome)
Villa Ruspoli, Vignanello

Lombardy
Castello Balduino, Montalto (Pavia)
Isola Bella, Lago Maggiore (Novara)

Veneto
Villa Barbarigo, Valsanzibio (Padua)
Villa Rizzardi, Pojega di Negrar (Verona)
Villa Pisani, Strà
Giardino Giusti, Verona

FRANCE
Château de Bagatelle, Paris
Château de Chenonceau, Chenonceau
Parc de Saint Cloud, Saint Cloud
Château de Vaux-le-Vicomte, Maincy
Château de Versailles, Versailles
Château de Villandry, Villandry
La Chèvre d'Or, Biot
Château du Pontrancart, Dieppe
La Garupe, Cap d'Antibes
La Mormaire, Paris

GREAT BRITAIN AND IRELAND
Chilham, Kent
Hampton Court, Herefordshire
Heslington Hall, Yorkshire
Hidcote Manor, Gloucestershire
Great Dixter, East Sussex
Levens Hall, Cumbria, Westmorland
Canons Ashby, Northants
Montacute House, Somersetshire
Elvaston, Derbyshire
Earlshall, Fifeshire
Cleeve Prior, Evesham
Sissinghurst Castle, Kent
Rochkingham Castle, Northamptonshire
Packwood House, Warwickshire
Cranborne Manor, Dorset
Howick Hall, Northumberland
Parnham, Dorset
Lanhydrook, Cornwall
St. Fagans, Ireland

HOLLAND
Beeckesteyn, Velsen
Hot Loo, Apeldoorn
De Wierden, Vorden
Weldam Castle, Goor
Twickel Garden, Delden
Warmelo, Diepenheim
Historical Gardens, Aaslemen
Canneman Neerlangbrock
De Haar in Haarzuilens
Zuylenstein Castle, Leersum

UNITED STATES
George Washington Garden, Mount Vernon, Virginia
Green Animals, Portsmouth, Rhode Island
Ladew Topiary Gardens, Monkton, Maryland
Villa Vizcaya, Florida

BELGIUM
Jardin de Belil, Tournai
Jardin Freier, Dinant
Gardens of Hearts, Brussels
Labyrinth Gardens, Brussels

SWEDEN
Clements Torq, Linnd
Ostra Kyrkogarde, Marno

DENMARK
Hirchholm Castle
Frederichsborg Castle

GERMANY
Weilburg Castle
Heidelberg Castle
Ludwingsburg Castle
Herrenhausen Gardens
Hermitage Palace, Bayreuth, Hannover

AUSTRIA
Schönbrunn Castle, Vienna
Wilhering Abbey

SPAIN
Alhambra, Granada
Alcázar, Seville
El Retiro, Madrid
Jardin de la Isla, Madrid

PORTUGAL
Palácio de Queluz, Lisbon
Palácio de Belém, Lisbon
Palácio dos Marqueses de Fronteira, Lisbon
Quinta (Donain) da Bacalhoa, Arrábida, Setúbal
Casa do Calhariz, Palmela, Setúbal
Queluz National Park, Lisbon
Casa da Insua, Penalva do Castelo, Coimbra
Solar (Manor) de Mateus, Mateus
Casa do Campo, Amarante, Oporto
Buçaco National Park
Palácio da Seteais, Sintra
Quinta do Palheiro, Madeira

Index

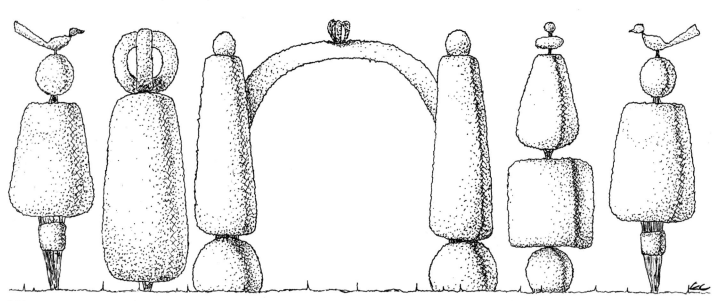